Day Skipper
Competent Crew

WILLIAM BARNES
RYA Instructor

Day Skipper
Competent Crew

STANFORD MARITIME

Published by Stanford Maritime
59 Grosvenor Street, London W1X 9DA

Photographs courtesy Yachting Monthly Library and W Whitfield, D Smyth,
P Roach, Guernsey Press, Ballena, D Forster and W Payne

Tidal curves Crown copyright. HMSO. Predictions computed by the Institute of
Oceanographic Sciences: copyright reserved.

British Library Cataloguing in Publication Data

Barnes, William
    Day skipper competent crew.
    1. Seamanship.   Navigation — For yachting
    I. Title
    623.89'0247971

    ISBN 0–540–07433–0

Printed in Great Britain by
Butler and Tanner Limited

Contents

Introduction

This book covers the aspects of a shore-based course of instruction for Day Skipper to RYA standards by addressing the theoretical aspects of seamanship and navigation. In addition to the book the student should study in depth and absorb the contents of the International Regulations for the Prevention of Collision at Sea, or RYA publication G2. Another important addition to the reader's library, is the Admiralty publication NP 5011 *Symbols and Abbreviations used on Admiralty Charts*, this will enable chart symbols to be interpreted.

The work is arranged so as to introduce the reader to the subject of seamanship and navigation in alternate packages. The reader will need some chartwork instruments in order to complete the exercises. It is important to work and re-work the exercises until the subject matter is thoroughly understood. Answers are given at the end of each chapter. The selection of instruments is a matter of choice, some guidance is however given in Chapter 3. Basically, a parallel rule, some dividers and a protractor will suffice, together with a supply of 2B pencils and a soft rubber. A non-metric chart of the Channel Islands, Stanford Chart no. 16 is provided with the book and this is adequate for all of the navigational exercises. The text covers metric charts and depth calculations, these are based upon the metric system.

This book has been developed over the years, starting as a few sheets handed out to Day Skipper students to clarify various points arising during the course, and gradually developing to a stage where it needed professional publication. Many of my past students may well recognise some of the text, and will groan. My thanks however are extended to them, for without their contribution and the difficulties that they experienced in grasping certain aspects of the subjects, this book may never have been written.

There is, however, a world of difference between a theoretical shore-based course of 'navigation and seamanship' and the real thing! One supplements the other, but there is no substitute for practical experience. It is hoped that this book will enable you not only to benefit from the learning and mistakes of others, but to be able to apply the theory with confidence and accuracy. Do not get disheartened by your inevitable mistakes, we have all made them and still occasionally do. The important this is, not to repeat them.

My own experience dates back to 1949 when in Berlin, I learned to sail with the RAF Boat Club at Gatow. Since then I have sailed off Hamburg, in mid-Pacific, off Australia, around the English South and East coasts and along the French and Belgian coasts. As an instructor I have taught both Day and Coastal Skippers and, like them, I am still learning. But one thing I have learnt is, that the sea does not suffer fools gladly. Be always careful and enjoy your sailing. Good luck!

Bill Barnes C ENG MIEE MIERE
Reading, Berks.

Navigation

The Importance of Navigation

Because of the dangers posed by rocks, unknown coastlines, other vessels, shoals etc; and because of hazards arising from strong winds or fog, it is most important in any vessel that your *position* is *known* at all times. The position of any point on the surface of the earth can be defined in terms of its latitude and longitude (always in that order).

Lines of Latitude

These can be likened to slices of the earth which are parallel to the equator. They are defined as a number of degrees and minutes north or south of the equator.

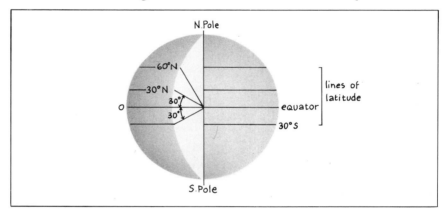

Lines of Longitude

These are imaginary lines, formed by the edges of circles, which run parallel to the axis of the poles. They effectively divide the earth into segments, much like an orange. They are defined as a number of degrees east or west of the Greenwich Meridian; this being a theoretical line that runs from the North to the South pole and which passes through London at Greenwich. The Greenwich Meridian is given the longitude of zero.

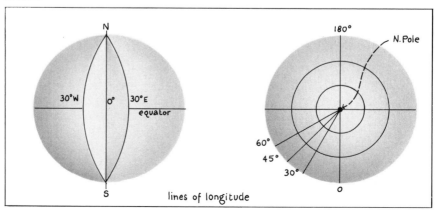

Position

A vessel's position is marked at frequent intervals (hourly) on a chart. A chart is effectively a diagram or plan of the seabed and coastline. It displays numerous features including depths, buoys, dangers and lighthouses. *It is **never** called a map!!*

The symbols used on charts are all listed and described in the Admiralty Chart NP 5011, *Symbols and Abbreviations used on Admiralty Charts*. It is necessary to study this document in depth.

Charts

The two major types of chart used for coastal navigation are Gnomic charts and Mercator charts. They are both produced by projections and are in effect distorted pictures of the surface of the Earth which enable bearings and courses to be accurately plotted. It may at first seem strange that a distorted picture is needed in order to produce an accurate plot! It is necessary however to have **flat** diagrams (charts) which consistently represent the curved surface of the Earth; these can only be produced by distortion (projection). A projection is the manner in which the picture of the Earth's surface is projected onto a flat surface.

Gnomic Charts

These are used for Polar navigation, Great Circle navigation and for large scale (more inches to the mile) charts of harbours.

A Gnomic chart could be imagined as the result of taking a thin slice from the surface of the earth and flattening it, much the same as a slice from a thin rubber ball might be flattened. On such a chart, lines of longitude converge and Great Circle tracks appear as straight lines.

Great Circle Tracks

A Great Circle is a slice through the earth whose plane passes through the Earth's centre. The shortest distance between two points on the Earth's surface is the arc of a Great Circle. By following a Great Circle track on long ocean voyages, considerable saving in distance travelled can be achieved.

Harbour plans and charts with a scale greater than 1 in 50,000 are also drawn using Gnomic projection where, over a small area, the Earth's surface can be considered to be flat.

Mercator Charts

Imagine a hollow transparent globe of the Earth with a point light source at its centre. Now place this globe inside a cylinder so that the features on the surface of the globe are projected onto the inside wall of the cylinder. If this image were then recorded and the surface of the cylinder rolled out flat, a distorted picture of the Earth's surface would be obtained whereby all the lines of longitude were parallel and the distance per degree between lines of latitude would increase towards the Poles. Such is the principle of a Mercator chart.

An important feature of a Mercator chart is, that because lines of longitude are shown as being parallel, a course set by fixed heading (true course) can be plotted as a straight line. Such lines are known as Rhumb lines and such charts are most useful for coastal navigation because angles, bearings and distances can be accurately represented.

Rhumb Lines

When a ship sails a constant **true** course, her fore and aft line cuts each successive meridian at the same angle. If one extends such a plot to a long ocean voyage, then

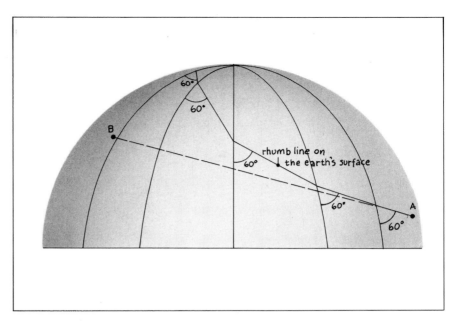

the effect of sailing on the surface of a sphere must be considered. The meridians are **not** parallel (except as depicted on a Mercator chart), they converge at the poles. Because of this, a rhumb line track which cuts each meridian at the same angle, will appear on the surface of the Earth as a spiral.

To sail the shortest distance between two points a great distance apart, a Great Circle track must be followed. A disadvantage of a Great Circle track is that since it cuts each meridian at a different angle, the course has to be altered day by day. In practice the navigator divides the Great Circle track into a series of rhumb line tracks, which together approximate to a Great Circle. Great Circle sailing is not normally used in coastal navigation.

Plane Sailing

Over a short distance, which should be less than about 600 miles, the Earth's surface, for practical navigation, can be assumed to be a plane, ie, a flat surface. This method of navigation is known as **plane sailing**.

Exercise 1

a Are lines of longitude parallel on the Earth's surface?
b Why is it necessary to measure distances of Mercator charts at the latitude of the plot?
c Why do rhumb lines appear as spiral tracks when plotted on the surface of the Earth?
d What is a Great Circle track?

Characteristics of Mercator charts

Latitude and Longitude The latitude scale is measured from either the left or right hand side of the chart. The longitudinal scale is measured from the top or the bottom of the chart. Scales are in degrees and minutes. Half minutes are used on large scale charts only.

A position is given in the following format:

50° 23'N 2°20'E

NB latitude is always given first.

Distances   These are always measured on the latitude scale and at the latitude at which the plot refers.

One minute of latitude = I nautical mile.
One cable = 1/10th of a nautical mile = 600 ft approx.

Courses and Bearings   The true (outer) compass rose is used to lay off courses or bearings on the chart. Use a *soft* pencil, 2B or softer. In chartwork only *true* courses or bearings should ever be plotted. Compass headings, used by the helmsman to steer the course must be converted to *true* courses before being plotted and vice versa.

Soundings   These are given in metres and are measured from chart datum. Chart datum refers to a theoretical level known as LAT (Lowest Astronomical Tide). In effect it ensures that the water level is never less than that shown on the chart. Some old charts may still be in use and these might well be scaled in fathoms and feet. Check before use.

Height of land features   These refer to the height above MHWS (Mean High Water Springs).

Variation   This is shown on the chart for the year in which it was drawn and needs to be updated for any calculations. Variation is the angle that a compass needle is deflected due to the difference between the position of the Magnetic North Pole and position of the True North Pole. It is measured in degrees and minutes, either east or west of True North. It varies with your position on the surface of the Earth and also from year to year. In the British Isles it is at present about 6° West and is decreasing.

Deviation   Magnetic deviation is the angle by which a compass needle is deflected by local magnetic fields within the vessel, it is caused by such things as the engine and the metal fittings. It is measured in degrees east or west and varies with the vessel's heading.

Corrections to Admiralty Charts and Publications   These are contained in the weekly Notices to Mariners and are obtainable from shipping offices. An annual summary is published together with a quarterly small craft edition. Charts can be updated by certain agents at a reasonable fee. They will rarely enter more than five corrections however. Amendments are entered in violet ink, they are never erased. The year and correction number is noted at the bottom left hand corner of the chart border.

Publications

A number of nautical publications in addition to charts are needed in order to navigate safely. These include:

Pilot books
Light lists
Tidal stream atlases
Nautical almanacs (*Reed's* or *Macmillan's*)
Mariner's handbooks
Merchant shipping notices

Exercise 2

a The inner magnetic rose on a chart is corrected for Variation. Can this be used to plot magnetic headings?
b What causes magnetic variation?
c What causes magnetic deviation? Is it a constant?
d How and from what information are corrections to charts made?

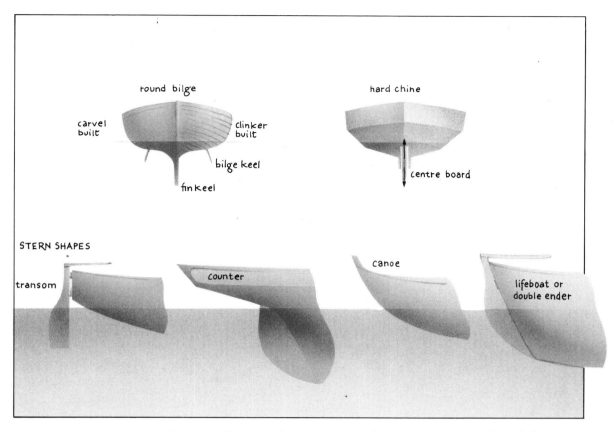

e Mark the Stanford Channel Island Chart supplied, in ink, as follows –

- On the Latitude scales at both sides of the chart, mark the scale at 5′ intervals and append the latitude as appropriate (eg 35′, 55′ etc.). This will simplify plotting at a later stage.
- Divide the distance on the scale between 48° 59′ and 49° into 5 equal parts. Mark the resulting graduations in ink.
- Mark the Longitude scale at the top of the chart at 2°W with a short line *above* the scale to align with the Meridian as drawn on the chart.

Hull forms

Round bilge hulls are favoured for slow displacement craft because of their better load carrying ability and easier motion in waves. The stability of a round bilge vessel however tends to decrease with speed.

Hard chine hulls have a higher speed potential than round bilge hulls and are capable of planing. They have however, a much harsher motion in head seas. This hull form usually requires a broad transom which makes control difficult in following seas.

Engines and seacocks

Diesel Engines Diesel engines are extremely reliable. Because they use a low volatile fuel they have a low fire risk. Running costs are low, but repairs and the initial costs are expensive. Their lower dependence upon electrics when running, makes them less likely to fail when subjected to the wet conditions encountered whilst sailing.

Petrol Engines   Petrol engines are cheaper to buy and install. They are lighter in weight, they create less vibration and with the exception of outboard motors, are quieter. They are additionally much easier for amateurs to maintain. The fuel used is more volatile, however.

Lubrication   Sump arrangements must enable oil to be pumped when the engine is tilted through large angles. (60° or more from the vertical).

Electrics   Electrics require to be adequately protected from the effects of moisture (humidity and spray).

Cooling   Components must be resistant to corrosion by sea water. Efficient filtering is required to separate weed and foreign matter from the cooling water and easy access for inspection and cleaning is required. Cooling water inlets and outlets require to be protected by seacocks.

Seacocks   These are valves fitted to all openings in the hull below or near the waterline. They enable the opening to be closed to prevent flooding or syphoning in the event of damage to hoses and fittings. They also enable maintenance and repair work to be undertaken whilst afloat and in addition, prevent water ingress during bad weather (large heeling angles) and seepage when the vessel is left unattended.

Parts of the hull

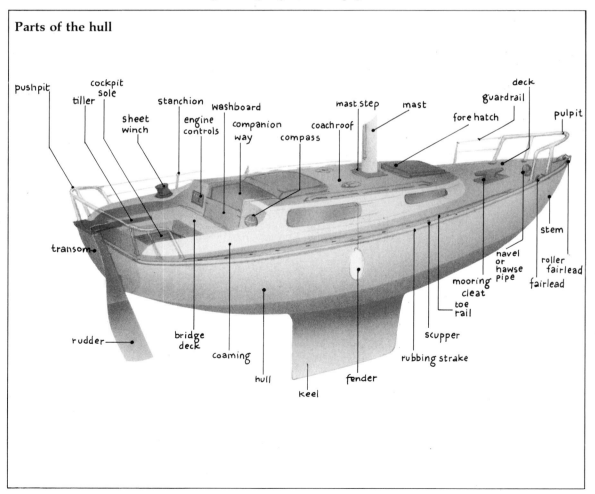

Rigs and riggings

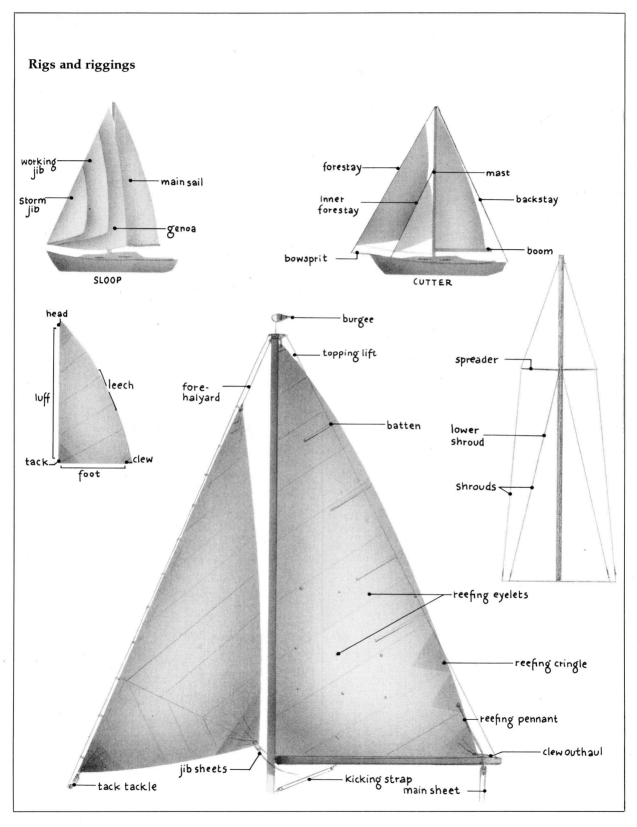

working jib

main sail

Storm jib

genoa

SLOOP

forestay

mast

inner forestay

backstay

bowsprit

boom

CUTTER

head

leech

luff

tack

clew

foot

burgee

topping lift

fore-halyard

batten

spreader

lower shroud

shrouds

reefing eyelets

reefing cringle

reefing pennant

clew outhaul

jib sheets

kicking strap

main sheet

tack tackle

Sailing terms

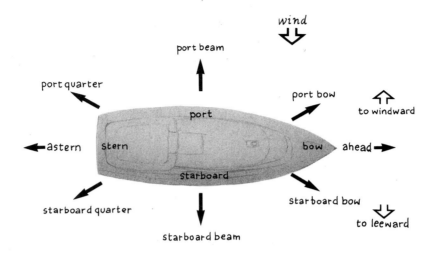

ON THE WIND = CLOSE HAULED   OFF THE WIND = NOT CLOSE HAULED

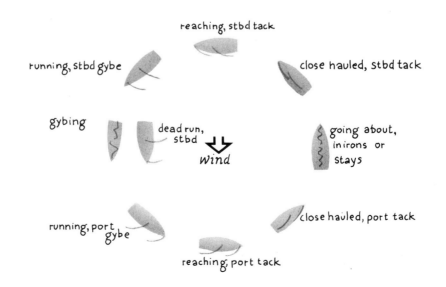

a Are round bilge hulls more stable at speed than hard chine hulls?

b List the advantages of marine diesel, over petrol, engines.

c Where and why are seacocks fitted?

Rigging and parts of the hull

There are two types of rigging used in a sailing vessel. Running rigging which enables the sails to be hoisted, lowered and trimmed to the wind and standing rigging which holds the masts and spars such as bowsprits rigidly in position. The names of the various parts of vessel's hull together with rigs, rigging and sailing terms are illustrated in the previous pages.

Exercise 4

a Give three examples of standing rigging.

b Which parts of a sail are known as the luff and the clew?

c Heading due North, from which direction is the wind, when on your port quarter?

d How close to a due North wind would you expect to sail, when close hauled on a starboard tack?

Answers to Chapter 1

Exercise 1

a No, they converge at the poles.

b Because the distance per degree between lines of latitude increases with latitude.

c Because they cut the successive meridians (lines of longitude) at the same angle. As the meridians converge, so will the rhumb line spiral towards the pole.

d The arc of a great circle and it is the shortest distance between two points on the Earth's surface.

Exercise 2

a It is bad practice to do so. The rose is only correct for the specified date.

b The difference in the positions of the Magnetic and True Poles.

c The influence of magnetic materials, in and within the hull of a vessel, upon her compass. No, it varies with the ships heading.

d Charts are corrected from information contained in Admiralty Notices to Mariners. Corrections are made using violet ink. The lower left hand border at the chart is marked with the year of issue and number of the appropriate notice.

Exercise 3

a No, they do not plane and some can yaw badly at speed.

b Reliable, less fire risk from the fuel, low running costs (but expensive to purchase initially), less likely to fail when wet.

c Fitted to hull openings below and close to the waterline to enable them to be closed to prevent flooding in the event of damage.

Exercise 4

a Main halyard, jib halyard, main sheet, jib sheet.

b Forward edge. Aftmost lower corner.

c South west.

d North west.

Compass

Compass Errors

A magnetic compass will not indicate the direction of True North. It indicates the direction of the Magnetic North Pole but, with an error caused by magnetic influences within the ship or boat.

Variation

If a vessel steers a constant compass course due north, she will eventually end up, not at the true North Pole but, at the North Magnetic Pole. The latter is located some distance away from the former.

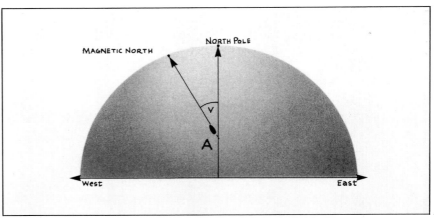

An error, known as variation, has occurred. If the error angle (v) were 5°, then it would be necessary, in this example, to steer a course of due north (magnetic) plus 5° to arrive at the North Pole. This is because from our starting position (A), the Magnetic Pole is 5° west of the True North Pole. The error in this case is labelled 5° west or variation (at A) = 5° west.

It follows therefore that to arrive at the North Pole, the compass course must be adjusted, by adding the variation error:

True course (N)	000° or 360°
Error	5° W
compass course to steer	005°

The variation gets larger closer to the Poles and in addition, at other longitudes, the other side of the Earth for instance, the Magnetic Pole lies to the *east* of true north.

With an easterly error it would be necessary to *subtract* the error, in order to achieve the desired course.

These facts must be remembered and applied when converting compass courses to true and vice versa. As an aid a useful mnemonic is:

Error West, Compass Best
Error East, Compass Least

ie if variation is west, then its value is **added** to the *true* course and the resulting value for the *compass* course is larger (best) than the true course value.

It follows that when converting compass to true, a west error is **subtracted** to fulfill the requirements, Error West, Compass Best.

Example – Compass to True

Compass course	175°C	
Variation	5°W	Error West, Compass best
True course	170°T	

Example – True to Compass

True course	273°T	
Variation	8°E	Error East, Compass least
Compass course	265°C	

Variation between True and Magnetic North varies from year to year and differs at various points on the Earth's surface. It is given on all charts as, so many degrees and minutes east or west for a given year.

Exercise 1

Convert the following courses from true to compass:

	True	Variation
a	180°T	5°W
b	250°T	8°W
c	010°T	3°W
d	155°T	5°E
e	357°T	7°E
f	005°T	9°E

Convert the following courses from compass to true:

	Compass	Variation
a	156°C	5°W
b	208°C	3°E
c	175°C	2°W
d	008°C	7°E
e	359°C	3°W

Deviation

A further error, deviation, occurs and is due to the effects of stray magnetic fields and electrical equipment within the vessel, upon the ships' compass. The errors are corrected in much the same way as for variation but, in converting from true to compass, variation errors are corrected first and then the deviation errors.

ie true to compass $T > V > M > D > C$

It follows that to convert from compass to true the corrections are done in the reverse order.

ie compass to true $C > D > M > V > T$

A common mnemonic used to remember this is:
Cadbury's Dairy Milk, Very Tasty

Example

Convert 061° compass to true. Deviation 3°E, variation 6°W.

Compass course	061°C	
Deviation	3°E	Error East
	064°M	(magnetic course)
Variation	6°W	Error West
True Course	058°T	

19

Complete the table below:

1	Compass	Deviation	Magnetic	Variation	True
a	025°C	6°W		6°W	
b	090°C	3°E		7°E	
c	180°C	5°W		4°W	
d	356°C		005°M		007 T
e	127°C		126°M		131 T

2	Compass	Deviation	Magnetic	Variation	True
a		4°W		6°W	059°T
b		7°W		3°E	357°T
c		2°E		4°W	187°T
d	093°C		086°M		091°T
e	348°C		356°M		001°T

Compass Errors and Plotting

Courses are always plotted as *true* directions and bearings. It is therefore essential to convert compass headings to true courses by making due allowance for the errors.

Compass Siting

When siting a compass the following points should be noted:

● The lubber line should be in line with the keel.

● Wiring near the compass should be twin wire. If not sure then test by switching on and off, to see if the compass is affected.

● Select a location near to the steering position and suitable for taking bearings.

● Avoid close proximity to electrical instruments.

● Keep other movable metal objects away from the compass.

● Have an oil or battery lamp handy for illumination.

Compass Swinging

Having sited the compass it is then necessary to determine the deviation errors. They vary with the ships heading and it is necessary to establish the error for all points of the compass and to draw up a deviation card. The simplest method is to check the steering compass against the hand bearing compass over a range of bearings at 22.5° intervals. This is known as compass swinging. This method of swinging however would not suffice in a magnetically complex vessel with steel rigging, rails and deck fittings. In such circumstances swing against defined transits or bearings.

Swinging should be undertaken at least once a year, preferably at the start of the season and particularly if any change in a major item of equipment has occurred, such as a new engine or rewiring job. A swing is also advised after a lightning strike although this is quite a rare occurrence. Swing with the engine running and again with the engine idle. While sailing, check deviations frequently with transits or the sun and check the error when the vessel is heeling (heeling error). The deviation card should be located near the compass.

Compass Correction

This is a specialised task and requires special equipment. Compensating magnets are positioned to reduce deviation errors. After such adjustment, the specialist should provide a deviation table and a note of the correction magnets fitted, together with their respective positions.

Exercise 3

a List four points to be considered when siting a compass.
b Is deviation a constant?
c What is compass swinging?
d Why is it necessary to convert compass headings to true courses?

Answers to Chapter 2

Exercise 1

1	**a** 185°C.	**b** 258°C.	**c** 013°C.	**d** 150°C.	**e** 350°C.	**f** 356°C.
2	**a** 151°T.	**b** 211°T.	**d** 173°T.	**d** 015°T.	**e** 356°T.	

Exercise 2

1	**a** 019°M, 013°T.	**b** 093°M, 100°T.	**c** 175°M, 171°T.
	d 9°E, 2°E.	**e** 1°W, 5°E.	
2	**a** 069°C, 065°M.	**b** 001°C, 354°M.	**c** 189°C, 191°M.
	7°W, 5°E.	**e** 8°E, 5°E.	

Exercise 3

a Lubber line aligned with keel, wiring twin wire, located near the steering position: avoid proximity to electrical equipment; remote from metal objects.
b No, it varies with heading.
c Method of determining deviation by comparing the ship's Compass heading with the heading indicated by a remote compass.
d To enable compass or magnetic bearings to be plotted as *true* courses or bearings, on a chart.

Pilotage, chartwork instruments and simple position fixing

Pilotage

This is the art of navigating safely in confined waters, such as when entering or leaving harbour. There is usually insufficient time to fix the vessels position from the chart under these conditions.

Pilotage relies heavily upon local knowledge, careful study of local charts, pilot books, sailing directions and some previously prepared notes of salient points.

Charts, sailing directions, tide tables and an echo sounder are used in pilotage together with binoculars, torch, lead-line, a barometer and a reliable clock. It is essential of course that all of the above equipment is in good working order and in the case of books and charts, of recent origin or update.

When entering difficult areas, do so on a **rising** tide. This will enable the vessel to be refloated should she run aground. It is essential to have a thorough knowledge of the local system of buoyage and a working knowledge of the *Rules of the Road*, particularly of those rules relating to lights and shapes.

Before entering or leaving harbour, you should try to have in your mind knowledge of the layout of the harbour and any hazards which may exist, together with the compass course that you wish to steer. At night it is also prudent to be aware of, and to have notes of, the lights that you might see and the order in which they are expected to be sighted. It is also necessary to study the tides and be aware of the manner in which they will affect your course and also to have knowledge of the expected weather conditions based upon the most recent forecast.

The use of outdated charts is not to be encouraged. Features on charts change quite frequently. Admiralty Notices to Mariners provide information enabling charts to be updated. There is also a Small Craft Edition for UK waters which is published quarterly at an approximate cost of £2.50.

When piloting a vessel it is essential to keep a sharp look-out at all times and to be constantly ready to take appropriate action to avoid danger. Under these circumstances it is not practical, on a sailing craft, to frequently go below to consult the chart. Nor is it sensible to risk the chart by bringing it up to the cockpit. Under these conditions the use of a notebook, in which to enter important details, is highly recommended. The notebook should contain information on buoyage, depths, tide streams and levels, point to point distances and courses. The notebook is not to be confused with the log-book.

Exercise 1

a How does pilotage differ from navigation?
b At what state of tide should you endeavour to enter difficult areas?
c List items of equipment, necessary for safe pilotage.
d What knowledge should be acquired before entering or leaving harbour?

Transits and Clearing Lines

These are lines of sight, set up on selected fixed objects. A transit line on a church and say a memorial ashore, might well enable a safe course to be steered in daylight on entering harbour. At night it is common for leading lights to be provided at ports and harbours. These are either kept in line, or a constant bearing maintained on them, to effect safe passage. Clearing lines are generally established as a bearing on an object beyond which it would not be safe to sail. Simple examples are given below.

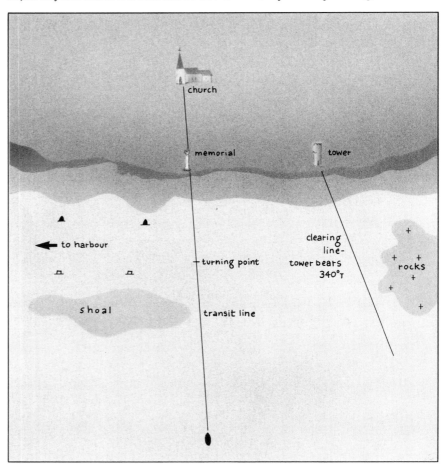

Logbook

The vessel's logbook or deck-log is a more formal document than a notebook. It should be 'made up' at frequent intervals. On long passages an hourly entry should suffice, on short coastal passages more frequent entries may be necessary.

The logbook entry should, as a minimum, record the time, the vessel's course and the log reading. It should additionally contain the barometric pressure and an estimate of the wind speed and direction. Intermediate entries, at the time at which they occur, should record information from which a positive **fix** can be obtained. It is good practice to plot a fix whenever the opportunity presents itself. When things go wrong, they have a tendency to go disastrously wrong, and in those circumstances a good reliable fix is a comforting asset.

Log entries must be clear and legible. Scribbled notes are useless to the next navigator coming on-watch, they are open to misinterpretation and are probably unreadable in conditions of poor light and or weather.

Logbooks are frequently illustrated with sketches of lighthouses, points of land or prominent features. Such a log can be interesting as well as informative and under some circumstances might also become a legal document in the event of a collision and subsequent claim for damages.

a What is a transit line and what is its purpose?
b What is the purpose of a clearing line?
c What are the minimum data for log book entry and how frequently should entries be made?

Chartwork instruments

Chartwork requires the use of certain basic instruments. There are many from which to choose, most have good and bad features. A basic engineering principle for good design has always been *keep it simple*!

On that basis I would recommend the following types of instruments:

- A 12in parallel rule, graduated with a protractor scale. (Captain Field's pattern)

- A 7in pair of single handed, bow type, dividers. These have a distinct advantage in that, by holding the bow in the palm of the hand and by placing the forefinger and thumb along the points, they can be opened by squeezing the bow in the palm, or closed by squeezing the points. This is most useful when you need your other hand to hold on. Remember, one hand for yourself and one for the boat!

- A 5in square protractor. (Douglas or similar).

- Two or three 2B pencils and a pencil sharpener. Don't use harder pencils, HB, H etc will score and cut the chart and erasing the lines is tricky.

- A soft rubber or eraser. Remember not to rub out lines on a *wet* chart.

The above items will, on a small yacht, be quite adequate for most requirements. The sizes are chosen as being suitable without being too large, bearing in mind the average size of a yacht's navigation table.

Now having selected the equipment, here are a few tips on how to make best use of it.

Parallel Rules   To lay-off a course or bearing with a parallel rule, most users start by lining up the rule on the compass rose, walking it to the required position and then draw the position line for the course. Unfortunately, what usually happens is that the rule slips during the walking process and a wrong bearing results or the process has to be repeated. It is much easier to align the south mark, on the lower edge of the rule, on a meridian close to the required position and then to rotate the rule until the required bearing on the upper edge is aligned with the same meridian. The rule is now parallel to the required bearing and is simply walked, over a much shorter distance, to the position and used to draw the required bearing line.

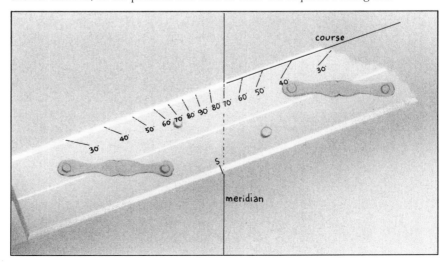

The rule can also be used to measure a bearing. To do this, align the rule on the bearing and then walk it to the nearest meridian. Position the south mark on the meridian and read off the bearing on the top scale. Be careful not to read off the reciprocal.

Square Protractor   The protractor can also be used to lay-off or measure bearings. Place the protractor with its central hole or mark precisely over your charted position, ensuring that the north mark on the protractor is *pointing north* and that the vertical lines on it are parallel to a meridian. Mark the chart with required bearing and then draw the position line through it.

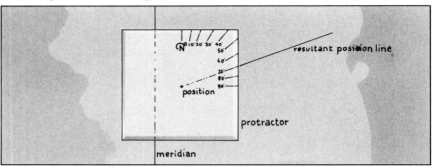

Bearings of lines are measured by positioning the protractor with its north mark pointing north and with its centre on the line. Adjust until the vertical lines on the protractor are parallel with a meridian and read off the bearing. Again, be careful not to read off the reciprocal. Most protractors give further instructions on other uses; the above are the basics.

Simple Position Fixing

The charted position of a vessel should be updated as frequently as her logbook, the one providing information for the other. If doubt as to an exact position exists, alter course away from the area of danger, if at all possible. The importance of determining your exact position cannot be overstressed when in shallow and dangerous water. If in doubt, heave to and try to work out just where you are.

Many factors contribute to the calculation of a position and failure of any one of these could give rise to some doubt. Hence the prudence of plotting a positive fix whenever the opportunity presents itself.

In plotting it is essential to convert compass bearings and to plot only **true** courses and bearings. My advice when learning to navigate for the first time is **never** use the magnetic compass rose on a chart. It is only accurate for a given date and is used as a datum for the calculation of variation in subsequent years.

There are now a number of good electronic aids available to determine accurately a vessel's position at sea. These are now widespread and people are beginning to doubt the necessity of learning to navigate. So be it, but electrical failures are not unknown in sailing craft and the prudent sailor could do worse than learn the art of navigation.

A vessel's position at sea can be found by dead reckoning (DR), by an estimated position (EP), or by a fix.

To Plot a lat/long Position – fix

This can be done using only a parallel rule, but the age-old problem of slipping can occur when walking the rule. It is easier using dividers and a parallel rule in the following manner:

First identify the intersection of a meridian and line of latitude (lat-line) nearest to your approximate position. Most charts are printed with about five meridians and five lat-lines in addition to the scales at each edge.

Then, with your dividers, measure the distance at the vertical edge of your chart (latitude scale) from your chosen lat-line to the required latitude (A in the diagram). Carefully transfer that measurement to the chosen intersection and mark off the **meridian** with a pencil at that distance.

Now measure, at the chart's horizontal edge (longitude scale), the distance from your chosen meridian to the required longitude (B). Carefully transfer that measurement to the intersection and mark off the distance along the chosen **lat-line**.

You now have two marks, close to your approximate position which correspond to the required latitude and longitude. It is a simple matter to transfer these, using the parallel rule, so that they intersect and thereby indicate the required position. The final position should be marked with a small circle around the intersection of these position lines.

If the dividers should slip, or the pencil marks be too heavy, some inaccuracies may occur using this method. Practice however, makes perfect!

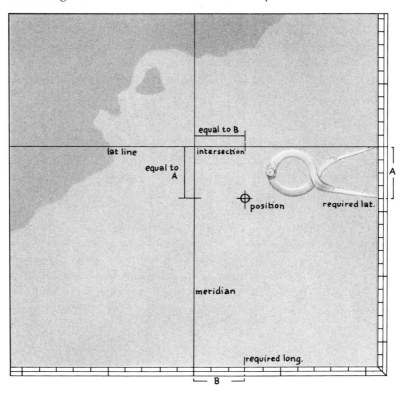

Example Using the Stanford Channel Islands Chart, plot the position 49° 4′ N 2° 36′W

Step 1   Identify a nearby intersection. Examination of the chart shows that the nearest meridian is 2° 40′ W, that the nearest lat-line is 49° N and that the approximate position is NE of the intersection.

Step 3   Measure the distance from the lat-line (49° N) to the required latitude (49° 4′ N). This distance is 4′ or 4 nautical miles. Mark off that distance on the 2° 40′ W meridian.

Step 3   Measure from the meridian (2° 40′ W) to the required longitude (2° 36′ W). This *length* is also 4′. (It is not however 4 miles. Remember, that *distances* are only measured along the latitude scale and, at the approximate latitude of your position. Mark off this length from the intersect and along the lat-line.

Step 4 Use the parallel rule to draw a horizontal line from the first mark and a vertical from the second. Mark their intersection with a small circle, thus:

Note. Your position should be alongside and just to the East of a note:

26

bk Sh G

This indicates that the depth at that point is 26 *fathoms* (Stanford Chart) and that the sea-bed consists of 'broken shells and gravel.'

Exercise 3

Stanford Chart

a What is the distance from the Position plotted in the example above, to the Meridian 2° 40′ W?

b Plot the position 49° 0.7′ N 2° 52.9 W. What is located there?

c What is the bearing of the Grand Lejon lighthouse (approx position 48° 45′ N 2° 40′ W) from the position you plotted at **b** above? What is the distance to the lighthouse?

Dead Reckoning

The position is determined by plotting from the last known position, the **true** course steered and marking off along that plot the distance sailed, as indicated by the patent log. A DR position is marked on the plot as a bar across the course and the time appended to it. A DR position makes **no** allowance for tidal drift.

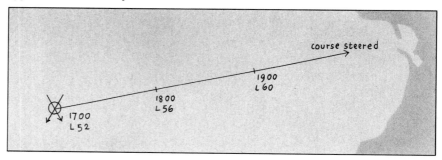

Estimated Position

An estimated position is effectively a DR position adjusted for tidal drift. It is shown on the chart as a triangle with the time appended. EPs will be studied in detail at a later stage.

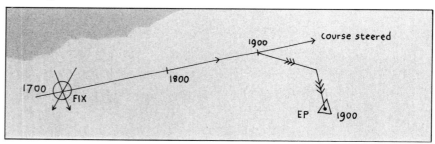

Fixed Position

This is marked on the chart as a small circle around the intersection of the lines upon which the fix was based and with the time of the fix appended. It indicates with certainty the *known* position at that time. There are a number of ways of establishing a fixed position and some of these are addressed below.

Exercise 4

a In shallow and dangerous waters, what action should be taken if your exact position is in doubt?
b What is the difference between a DR and an EP?
c How is a fixed position drawn on a chart?

Absolute Fix

This is obtained by taking simultaneous bearings of two or more *fixed* navigational marks. The intersection of the resulting position lines gives the vessel's position. Uncertainty of the fix is indicated by the area covered by the triangle arising from three such position lines. This area is known as a 'cocked hat'.

An absolute fix can also be obtained from a single bearing and an accurate 'distance off'. Distance off being determined by a vertical sextant angle on an object of known height or alternatively, a sharply defined discontinuity on the sea bed.

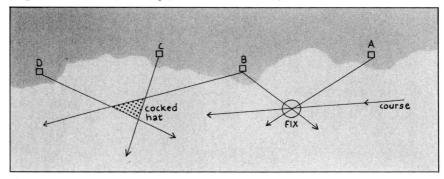

Running Fix

This is obtained by taking a bearing on a fixed object and then after maintaining a fixed and steady course for a logged distance, taking a further bearing on the same object. The position is determined by first plotting the position lines for the two bearings then, from any point on the first position line, plotting the true course steered; mark off the 'distance run' along that course and then draw a line through that point and parallel to the first position or bearing line. Your position is the point where this line, identified by double arrow heads at each end, intercepts the second position line. The diagram below illustrates the process.

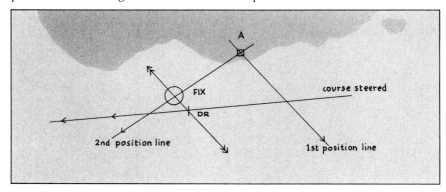

Doubling the Angle on the Bow

Using this procedure, first take a bearing *relative to the vessel's head* on a fixed object. Then maintain a fixed and steady course until the bearing of the object, relative to the ship's head, or 'off the bow' has doubled, note the distance run at that time. Your fixed position then lies along the second position line at a 'distance off' from the fixed object equal to the distance run between taking the first and second bearings. The procedure is illustrated below.

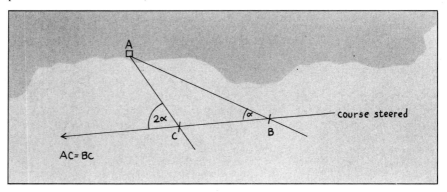

It is to be noted that the above methods make no allowance for tide or leeway and as such are simple methods of fixing a position, very much akin to a DR position. The procedure to be adopted to allow for tidal streams will be addressed later.

Exercise 5

a Describe two methods of obtaining an absolute fix.
b What is a cocked hat?
c Name two methods of obtaining a fix from a single object ashore.

Exercise 6

Stanford Chart
a Sorel Pt LH (lighthouse – N Jersey) bears 145°T and Banc Desormes buoy (W Cardinal) bears 220°T. What is your position?
b St Martins Pt LH (Guernsey) bears 028°T and is 11.6M (miles) from your position. What is your position?
c At 0900 a vessel is steering 260°T at 4 Knots and La Corbiere LH (SW Jersey) bears 330°T. At 1100 La Corbiere bears 035°T. What is her position at 1100? (Running fix problem).
d At 1115 a vessel is steering 345°T at 7.5 kts; Grosnez Pt LH (NW Jersey) lies 40° off the starboard bow. At 1215 Grosnez Pt lies 80° off the starboard bow. What is her position at 1215? (Double the angle off the bow problem).

Answers to Chapter 3

Exercise 1
a Pilotage is the art of navigating safely in confined waters, when there is insufficient time to *fix* a vessel's position from a chart.
b On a rising tide.
c Charts, sailing directions, tide tables and an echo sounder.
d Weather conditions, tide state, harbour layout, buoyage, hazards and course to steer.

Exercise 2
a A line of sight on a fixed object, to enable a safe course to be steered.
b To establish a line, beyond which it is unsafe to sail.
c Time, course, log and barometer readings. Hourly.

Exercise 3
a 2.8M
b Buoy V Qk F1 (9) 10s Whis (A West Cardinal buoy)
c 151°T. 17.8M (remember, distance is measured on the latitude scale).

Exercise 4

a Alter course away from the area of danger or heave-to and establish your position.

b An EP takes account of the effects of tidal drift.

c With a small circle around the intersection of the lines upon which the fix was based and with the time of the fix appended.

Exercise 5

a Simultaneous intersecting bearings on two or more *fixed* navigational marks. A single bearing on a 'mark' and an accurate 'distance off'.

b An uncertainty of fix indicated by a triangle arising at the intersection of three bearings or position lines.

c Running fix. Doubling the angle on the bow.

Exercise 6

a 49° 21.1′N; 2° 15.3′W.

b 49° 15′N; 2° 40′W.

c 49° 4.2′N; 2° 22.1′W (NB. 2 hour vector ∴ distance run = 8M).

d 49° 12.3′N; 2° 25′W.

Ropes and ropework

Rope is made from natural or synthetic fibres twisted into strands. Ropemaking is an ancient and highly specialised craft. The most widely used ropes consist of three strands which are laid up to form a right-handed or 'hawser-laid' rope. Ropes should be coiled correctly and kept free of kinks. They should be protected from chafe and when wear has occurred, turned end for end, to prolong their life. In use it is important to use the *correct* bends and hitches and to avoid bends over small radii. The strength of a rope is significantly reduced when sharply bent. Loads on ropes should preferably be steady; sharp jerks can lead to failure. The ends of all ropes should be properly finished by either whippings or, in the case of synthetic ropes by fusing the ends. Ropes should be clean and properly coiled when stored.

Types of rope

Natural Fibre Ropes   These are made from hemp, sisal, cotton or coir. They can be used generally wherever synthetic ropes are used but, they do have limitations. They are not as strong, they absorb water and swell and can be difficult to untie when wet. They do however stretch, rarely give way without warning and are ideal for tuition and practice in the 'mystic art' of tying knots, hitches, bends and splices.

Synthetic Ropes   *Types and Uses.* Synthetic ropes are made from nylon, terylene and polypropylene. Terylene ropes are used for halyards and sheets because they do not stretch. Nylon ropes are used for anchor warps because they do stretch. Braided or plaited terylene ropes are particularly suitable for sheets which are to be handled by winches. They are, however, very difficult to splice. Polypropylene rope is buoyant and very suitable for towing purposes.

Advantages. They do not absorb moisture and therefore do not become stiff when wet. With the exception of nylon, they also retain their strength when wet. They do not rot and they have a much longer useful life than natural ropes.

Disadvantages. They give no audible warning prior to breaking, and tend to break suddenly and with considerable whip-lash. They are more 'slippery' than natural ropes and require careful handling. (Three turns around a winch are generally necessary with synthetic ropes and riding turns are difficult to release.)

Knots and their uses

A **bend** is used for joining the ends of two ropes.

A **hitch** secures a rope to another object.

Figure of Eight   Used to prevent the end of a line running out through an eye or a block.

Clove Hitch   Used to secure a rope to spar, eg securing fenders temporarily to a guard rail, or a halyard to a burgee staff. It can also be tied with a loop in the final turn, enabling quick release for temporary use.

Rolling Hitch   Similar to a clove hitch but with an extra turn round the spar. Used to take the strain along a spar. Very useful to take the strain off a sheet in the event of a winch jamming or other lines fouling.

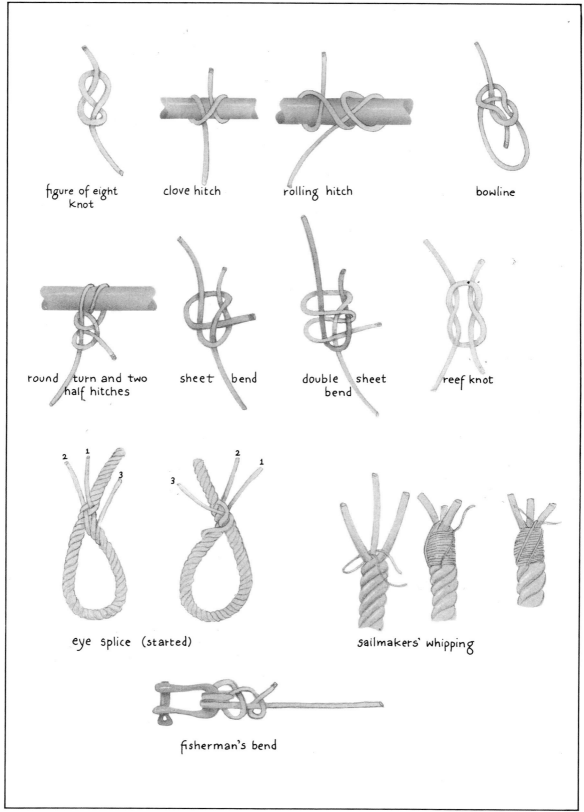

figure of eight
knot

clove hitch

rolling hitch

bowline

round turn and two
half hitches

sheet bend

double sheet
bend

reef knot

eye splice (started)

sailmakers' whipping

fisherman's bend

Bowline   Used to make a temporary loop or an eye that will not slip. There are many ways of tying a bowline quickly, some of these should be learnt and practised. If two bowlines are joined to extend a rope, the loops should be cow-hitched together to reduce wear.

Round Turn and Two Half Hitches   Used to secure a rope under strain. Can be used to secure fenders or ropes to rings or shackles. A round turn enables very good control when paying out a line under strain.

Sheet Bend   Used for joining two ropes of unequal size. A double sheet bend should be used when joining synthetic ropes; this bend is also useful for joining two tow ropes to extend the length. For more permanent use the end should be seized.

Reef Knot   Used for joining two ropes of equal thickness. The description originates from its use in tying reefing points.

Eyesplice   Used to make a permanent loop or eye in a rope. A thimble is secured in the eye when a rope is secured to a cable by a shackle.

Sailmakers Whipping   Used to prevent the strands of a three-strand rope unravelling. It does not come undone as easily as a plain whipping.

Fishermans Bend   Used for securing a warp to an anchor ring. It is prudent to seize the bitter end to the standing part to prevent the knot from working loose as the vessel swings, with the tide, to her anchor.

Belaying a Rope (securing to cleat)   A round turn should first be taken round the cleat and then a sufficient number of figure of eight turns made up to prevent slippage. It is common practice to invert the last one or two turns (locking hitches) when making up for an overnight stay for instance. When using synthetic ropes locking hitches are essential to prevent slippage.

Exercise 1

Which knot should be used for:

a Securing a mooring warp to a ring?
b To join two ropes of unequal thickness?
c To form a loop that will not slip?
d To secure a rope under strain?
e To take the strain off a sheet jammed on a winch?
f To join polypropylene ropes?

Mooring

Mooring Alongside   When approaching a berth, be particularly aware of the speed and direction of the wind and tide. Keep clear of overhanging obstructions and look out for warnings and underwater obstructions. If you intend to take the ground, be sure that the seabed is free from obstructions and reasonably level. When mooring alongside another craft, provide adequate fenders and avoid lining up your mast with that of the other vessel; in the event of heavy weather or wash from a passing vessel, it is not unknown for the masts of adjacent vessels to collide. Ensure that you take fore and aft warps ashore; do not rely on other vessels lines.

When mooring overnight on a large tidal range, fore and aft breast ropes to a fixed jetty will require frequent attention. All warps will probably require to be eased or taken up, as they become strained or slackened. Remember that the main strain is taken by the head warp and the back spring, when a vessel is lying with her head to the tide.

When using bowlines to tie up to a bollard, be sure to pass your bowline up and through the bowlines or 'eyes' of any other warps on that bollard. This will enable other yachts to be cast off individually, when the need arises, without untying other warps.

Positions of Mooring Ropes   In general mooring ropes should be positioned as shown below. The identities and functions of the individual warps are as follows:

1	head warp	These share the main load with 3 & 4.
2	stern warp	
3 & 4	fore and aft breast ropes	These hold the vessel alongside and share the main load.
5	head spring	The springs prevent surge, ie move-ment to and fro.
6	back spring	

The minimum length of a spring should be 3–5 times the tidal range if the vessel is to be moored for a tidal cycle.

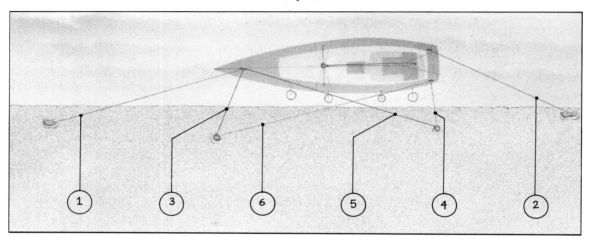

Exercise 2

When mooring alongside another vessel, list the actions and precautions that must be taken.

Answers to Chapter 4

Exercise 1
a Round turn and two half hitches.
b Sheet bend
c Bowline.
d Round turn and two half hitches.
e Rolling hitch.
f Double sheet bend.

Exercise 2
Ask permission to moor alongside, provide adequate fenders, provide mooring lines fore and aft, springs, and lines to the shore, position your vessel to avoid masts colliding in a heavy seaway.

Recognition and visibility of lights

Navigation lights

Recognition of Lights   It is important to be able to recognise a vessel's function at night and to determine with certainty her heading. To ensure this, vessels are required to display specific arrangements of navigation lights. Lights should be displayed from sunset to sunrise, and as necessary during daylight hours. The general positions and definitions for these lights are listed below. It is not proposed to describe in detail the various arrangements of lights, these are most adequately addressed in RYA Publication G2.

Positions of Lights   The positions and visible angles for navigation lights are illustrated in the diagram below.

Masthead Lights	Side lights	Sternlight
WHITE 225°	RED/GREEN 112.5°	WHITE 135°
(aft higher than fore)		

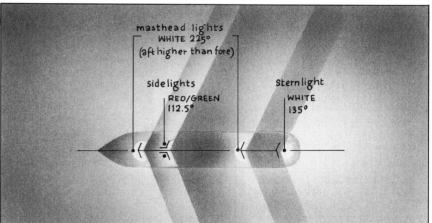

Definitions of Lights

Masthead Light   White. Must be visible from dead ahead to 22.5° abaft the beam, ie arc 225°

Sidelights   Red or Green. Must be visible from dead ahead to 22.5° abaft either the port or starboard beam, ie arc 112.5°.

Sternlight   White. Must be visible from dead astern to 22.5° abaft the beam, ie arc 135°.

Towing Light   A **yellow** light having the same characteristics as a stern light but mounted above it.

All Round Light   A light showing an unbroken light over a 360° arc.

Flashing Light   A light flashing at 120 flashes or more per minute.

Lights to be Carried by Vessels Underway

A vessel is said to be underway when she is not at anchor, aground, or made fast to the shore.

Motor vessels

Vessels 12–20 m Length overall (LOA)
Masthead Light   (2.5 m above the sidelights) visible 3 M.
Sidelights   (can be combined) visible 2 M
Sternlight   visible 2 M

Vessels less than 12 m LOA
Masthead light   (1 m above sidelight) visible 2 M
Sidelights   (can be combined) visible 1 M
Sternlight   (can be combined with masthead light) visible 2 M

Vessels less than 7 m LOA (Max speed 7 knots)
All round white light (ie combined masthead light and sternlight) visible 2 M. Sidelights should be carried if practical.

The minimum ranges quoted refer to conditions on a dark clear night, ie Met. visibility of 13 miles.

Sailing yachts

Vessels under sail are required to carry only sidelights and a sternlight. These can, for vessels less than 20 m LOA, be combined in a single tricolour lantern at the masthead, thereby reducing battery drain. A sailing vessel may also show an all-round red over an all-round green at the masthead, but these are optional and seldom fitted.

When motoring, lights appropriate to a power driven vessel must be displayed and provision must be made to carry both sets of lights.

Vessels less than 20 m LOA under sail
Tricolour lantern at the masthead
or sidelights (can be combined) and sternlight.

Vessels less than 12 m LOA
Tricolour lantern at the masthead
or sidelights (can be combined) and sternlight.

Under power
An independently switched (from the tricolour) all-round white light mounted beneath the tricolour can provide the requirements of masthead and stern lights and a combined sidelight lantern on the bow completes the requirements.

NB If both tricolour and a combined sidelight lantern on the bow are fitted, it is important to ensure that both are **never** displayed together.
Small Craft at Anchor Such craft should display an all-round white light.

Visibility of Lights

Light	Length of vessel and minimum visibility		
	Under 12 m	12–50 m	50 m and over
Masthead	2 M	5 M (3 M vessels greater than 12 m & less than 20 m)	6 M
Sidelight	1 M	2 M	3 M
Sternlight	1 M	2 M	3 M
Towing light	2 M	2 M	3 M
All-round lights	2 M	2 M	3 M

Recognition of Lights

The lights displayed by vessels at night fall into two categories:

a Those which indicate the vessel's heading (masthead, side and stern lights) and,

b those which describe her function.

Those in group **a** are (with the exception of the combined masthead, side and stern light of a sailing vessel under power) all sectored lights. These enable the vessel's **heading** to be determined with some certainty.

The lights in group **b** are with the notable exception of a vessel towing, mainly **all-round** lights. These enable the vessel's **function** to be determined with certainty, regardless of the angle of approach.

Towing vessels display one, or two, additional sectored masthead lights, depending upon the length of the tow. A tow is measured from the *stern* of the towing vessel to the *stern* of the last vessel in the tow.

It is most important at night to be able to determine a vessel's heading in order that appropriate and early action can be taken to avoid collision. The extent of the avoiding action is determined by recognition of the other vessel's function.

The recognition of lights and their significance is simplified by adopting the following procedure:

Firstly, establish her *heading* by concentrating on:

● the masthead and either the port or starboard lights, or

● the stern light.

Secondly, identify her *function*; restricted in her ability to manoeuvre, dredger, trawler etc.

Finally, in the case of dredgers, trawlers and fishing vessels, determine the direction of outlying gear, if any.

Exercise 1

a Between what times must navigation lights be displayed?
b What is the arc of visibility of a port navigation light?
c What type of vessels display a yellow sectored light over the stern light?
d What lights should a sailing vessel less than 12 metres in length, display?

Dipping Distances

The dipping distance is the distance from the observer to the horizon, ignoring visibility. It is mainly governed by the height of the observer. The curvature of the earth limits the visible range to the horizon and this distance increases with the height

Table 1: Distance of sea horizon in nautical miles

Height in metres	Height in feet	Distance in miles	Height in metres	Height in feet	Distance in miles	Height in metres	Height in feet	Distance in miles	Height in metres	Height in feet	Distance in miles
0.3	1	1.15	4.3	14	4.30	12.2	40	7.27	55	180	15.4
0.6	2	1.62	4.9	16	4.60	12.8	42	7.44	61	200	16.2
0.9	3	1.99	5.5	18	4.87	13.4	44	7.62	73	240	17.8
1.2	4	2.30	6.1	20	5.14	14.0	46	7.79	85	280	19.2
1.5	5	2.57	6.7	22	5.39	14.6	48	7.96	98	320	20.5
1.8	6	2.81	7.3	24	5.62	15.2	50	8.1	110	360	21.8
2.1	7	3.04	7.9	26	5.86	18	60	8.9	122	400	23.0
2.4	8	3.25	8.5	28	6.08	20	70	9.6	137	450	24.3
2.7	9	3.45	9.1	30	6.30	24	80	10.3	152	500	25.7
3.0	10	3.63	9.8	32	6.50	27	90	10.9	183	600	28.1
3.4	11	3.81	10.4	34	6.70	30	100	11.5	213	700	30.4
3.7	12	3.98	11.0	36	6.90	40	130	13.1	244	800	32.5
4.0	13	4.14	11.6	38	7.09	46	150	14.1			

of the observer. If the observer's height is known, the visible distance can be calculated. Most almanacs provide tables in which the distances for given heights are calculated. Table 1 is an example of such a table taken from the Reeds Almanac, the manner in which this is used is explained in the following example.

Example

If the eye of an observer is 5 ft (1.5 m), the horizon distance, from the table, is 2.57 miles. Similarly for a height of 10 ft, the distance to the horizon is 3.63 miles.

It is also possible to see objects such as lighthouses and large vessels when they are **over** the horizon, and moreover, if their **height above sea level** is known, to determine how far away they are.

By way of example, consider the following:

An observer A is 5 ft above sea level and can see a point P on the horizon 2.57 miles away. Another observer B is 10 ft above sea level and can see the same point 3.63

Table 2: To find distance off lights rising or dipping

Height of Light		Height of eye												
		Metres												
		1.5	3	4.6	6.1	7.6	9.1	10.7	12.2	13.7	15.2	16.8	18.3	19.8
		Feet												
		5	10	15	20	25	30	35	40	45	50	55	60	65
m	ft													
12	40	$9\frac{3}{4}$	11	$11\frac{1}{4}$	$12\frac{1}{2}$	13	$13\frac{1}{2}$	14	$14\frac{1}{2}$	15	$15\frac{1}{2}$	$15\frac{3}{4}$	$16\frac{1}{4}$	$16\frac{1}{2}$
15	50	$10\frac{3}{4}$	$11\frac{1}{4}$	$12\frac{1}{2}$	$13\frac{1}{4}$	14	$14\frac{1}{2}$	15	$15\frac{1}{2}$	$15\frac{3}{4}$	$16\frac{1}{4}$	$16\frac{3}{4}$	17	$17\frac{1}{2}$
18	60	$11\frac{1}{2}$	$12\frac{1}{2}$	$13\frac{1}{2}$	14	$14\frac{3}{4}$	$15\frac{1}{4}$	$15\frac{3}{4}$	$16\frac{1}{4}$	$16\frac{1}{2}$	17	$17\frac{1}{2}$	$17\frac{3}{4}$	$18\frac{1}{4}$
21	70	$12\frac{1}{4}$	$13\frac{1}{4}$	14	$14\frac{3}{4}$	$15\frac{1}{2}$	16	$16\frac{1}{2}$	17	$17\frac{1}{4}$	$17\frac{3}{4}$	18	$18\frac{1}{2}$	19
24	80	13	14	$14\frac{3}{4}$	$15\frac{1}{2}$	16	$16\frac{1}{2}$	17	$17\frac{1}{2}$	18	$18\frac{1}{2}$	$18\frac{3}{4}$	$19\frac{1}{4}$	$19\frac{1}{2}$
27	90	$13\frac{1}{2}$	$14\frac{1}{2}$	$15\frac{1}{4}$	16	$16\frac{3}{4}$	$17\frac{1}{4}$	$17\frac{3}{4}$	$18\frac{1}{4}$	$18\frac{1}{2}$	19	$19\frac{1}{2}$	$19\frac{3}{4}$	$20\frac{1}{4}$
30	100	14	15	16	$16\frac{1}{2}$	$17\frac{1}{4}$	$17\frac{3}{4}$	$18\frac{1}{4}$	$18\frac{3}{4}$	$19\frac{1}{4}$	$19\frac{1}{2}$	20	$20\frac{1}{2}$	$20\frac{3}{4}$
34	110	$14\frac{1}{2}$	$15\frac{3}{4}$	$16\frac{1}{2}$	$17\frac{1}{4}$	$17\frac{3}{4}$	$18\frac{1}{4}$	19	$19\frac{1}{4}$	$19\frac{3}{4}$	$20\frac{1}{4}$	$20\frac{1}{2}$	21	$21\frac{1}{4}$
37	120	$15\frac{1}{4}$	$16\frac{1}{4}$	17	$17\frac{3}{4}$	$18\frac{1}{4}$	19	$19\frac{1}{2}$	20	$20\frac{1}{4}$	$20\frac{3}{4}$	21	$21\frac{1}{2}$	22
40	130	$15\frac{3}{4}$	$16\frac{3}{4}$	$17\frac{1}{2}$	$18\frac{1}{4}$	19	$19\frac{1}{2}$	20	$20\frac{1}{2}$	$20\frac{3}{4}$	$21\frac{1}{4}$	$21\frac{1}{2}$	22	$22\frac{1}{2}$
43	140	$16\frac{1}{4}$	$17\frac{1}{4}$	18	$18\frac{3}{4}$	$19\frac{1}{2}$	20	$20\frac{1}{2}$	21	$21\frac{1}{4}$	$21\frac{3}{4}$	22	$22\frac{1}{2}$	23
46	150	$16\frac{3}{4}$	$17\frac{3}{4}$	$18\frac{1}{2}$	$19\frac{1}{4}$	$19\frac{3}{4}$	$20\frac{1}{2}$	21	$21\frac{1}{4}$	$21\frac{3}{4}$	$22\frac{1}{4}$	$22\frac{1}{2}$	23	$23\frac{3}{4}$
49	160	17	$18\frac{1}{4}$	19	$19\frac{3}{4}$	$20\frac{1}{4}$	$20\frac{3}{4}$	$21\frac{1}{2}$	$21\frac{3}{4}$	$22\frac{1}{4}$	$22\frac{3}{4}$	23	$23\frac{1}{2}$	$23\frac{3}{4}$
52	170	$17\frac{1}{2}$	$18\frac{1}{2}$	$19\frac{1}{2}$	20	$20\frac{3}{4}$	$21\frac{1}{4}$	$21\frac{3}{4}$	$22\frac{1}{4}$	$22\frac{3}{4}$	23	$23\frac{1}{2}$	24	$24\frac{1}{4}$
55	180	18	19	20	$20\frac{1}{2}$	$21\frac{1}{4}$	$21\frac{3}{4}$	$22\frac{1}{4}$	$22\frac{3}{4}$	23	$23\frac{1}{2}$	24	$24\frac{1}{4}$	$24\frac{3}{4}$
58	190	$18\frac{1}{2}$	$19\frac{1}{2}$	$20\frac{1}{4}$	21	$21\frac{1}{2}$	22	$22\frac{3}{4}$	23	$23\frac{1}{2}$	24	$24\frac{1}{2}$	$24\frac{3}{4}$	25
61	200	$18\frac{3}{4}$	20	$20\frac{3}{4}$	$21\frac{1}{2}$	22	$22\frac{1}{2}$	23	$23\frac{1}{2}$	24	$24\frac{1}{4}$	$24\frac{3}{4}$	$25\frac{1}{4}$	$25\frac{1}{2}$
64	210	$19\frac{1}{4}$	$20\frac{1}{4}$	21	$21\frac{3}{4}$	$22\frac{1}{4}$	23	$23\frac{1}{2}$	24	$24\frac{1}{4}$	$24\frac{3}{4}$	$25\frac{1}{4}$	$25\frac{1}{2}$	26
67	220	$19\frac{1}{2}$	$20\frac{3}{4}$	$21\frac{1}{2}$	$22\frac{1}{4}$	$22\frac{3}{4}$	$23\frac{1}{4}$	24	$24\frac{1}{4}$	$24\frac{3}{4}$	$25\frac{1}{4}$	$25\frac{1}{2}$	26	$26\frac{1}{4}$
70	230	20	21	22	$22\frac{1}{2}$	$23\frac{1}{4}$	$23\frac{3}{4}$	$24\frac{1}{4}$	$24\frac{3}{4}$	25	$25\frac{1}{2}$	26	$26\frac{1}{4}$	$26\frac{3}{4}$
73	240	$20\frac{1}{2}$	$21\frac{1}{2}$	$22\frac{1}{4}$	23	$23\frac{1}{2}$	24	$24\frac{1}{2}$	25	$25\frac{1}{2}$	26	$26\frac{1}{4}$	$26\frac{3}{4}$	27
76	250	$20\frac{3}{4}$	$21\frac{3}{4}$	$22\frac{1}{2}$	$23\frac{1}{4}$	24	$24\frac{1}{4}$	25	$25\frac{1}{2}$	26	$26\frac{1}{4}$	$26\frac{3}{4}$	27	$27\frac{1}{2}$
79	260	21	$22\frac{1}{4}$	23	$23\frac{3}{4}$	$24\frac{1}{4}$	$24\frac{3}{4}$	$25\frac{1}{4}$	$25\frac{3}{4}$	$26\frac{1}{4}$	$26\frac{3}{4}$	27	$27\frac{1}{2}$	$27\frac{3}{4}$
82	270	$21\frac{1}{2}$	$22\frac{1}{2}$	$23\frac{1}{4}$	24	$24\frac{1}{2}$	$25\frac{1}{4}$	$25\frac{3}{4}$	$26\frac{1}{4}$	$26\frac{1}{2}$	27	$27\frac{1}{2}$	$27\frac{3}{4}$	$28\frac{1}{4}$
85	280	$21\frac{1}{4}$	23	$23\frac{3}{4}$	$24\frac{1}{2}$	25	$25\frac{1}{2}$	26	$26\frac{1}{2}$	27	$27\frac{1}{2}$	$27\frac{3}{4}$	28	$28\frac{1}{2}$
88	290	22	$23\frac{1}{4}$	24	$24\frac{3}{4}$	$25\frac{1}{4}$	26	$26\frac{1}{2}$	$26\frac{3}{4}$	$27\frac{1}{4}$	$27\frac{3}{4}$	28	$28\frac{1}{2}$	$28\frac{3}{4}$
91	300	$22\frac{1}{2}$	$23\frac{1}{2}$	$24\frac{1}{2}$	25	$25\frac{3}{4}$	$26\frac{1}{4}$	$26\frac{3}{4}$	$27\frac{1}{4}$	$27\frac{1}{2}$	28	$28\frac{1}{4}$	$28\frac{3}{4}$	$29\frac{1}{4}$
95	310	$22\frac{3}{4}$	24	$24\frac{3}{4}$	$25\frac{1}{2}$	26	$26\frac{1}{2}$	27	$27\frac{1}{2}$	28	$28\frac{1}{2}$	$28\frac{3}{4}$	29	$29\frac{1}{2}$
98	320	23	$24\frac{1}{4}$	25	$25\frac{3}{4}$	$26\frac{1}{4}$	27	$27\frac{1}{2}$	$27\frac{3}{4}$	$28\frac{1}{4}$	$28\frac{3}{4}$	29	$29\frac{1}{2}$	$29\frac{3}{4}$
100	330	$23\frac{1}{2}$	$24\frac{1}{2}$	$25\frac{1}{4}$	26	$26\frac{1}{2}$	$27\frac{1}{4}$	$27\frac{3}{4}$	28	$28\frac{1}{2}$	29	$29\frac{1}{2}$	$29\frac{3}{4}$	30
104	340	$23\frac{3}{4}$	$24\frac{3}{4}$	$25\frac{1}{2}$	$26\frac{1}{4}$	27	$27\frac{1}{2}$	28	$28\frac{1}{2}$	29	$29\frac{1}{4}$	$29\frac{3}{4}$	30	$30\frac{1}{2}$
107	350	24	25	26	$26\frac{3}{4}$	$27\frac{1}{4}$	$27\frac{3}{4}$	$28\frac{1}{4}$	$28\frac{3}{4}$	$29\frac{1}{4}$	$29\frac{1}{2}$	30	$30\frac{1}{2}$	$30\frac{3}{4}$
122	400	$25\frac{1}{2}$	$26\frac{1}{2}$	$27\frac{1}{2}$	28	$28\frac{3}{4}$	$29\frac{1}{4}$	$29\frac{3}{4}$	$30\frac{1}{4}$	$30\frac{3}{4}$	31	$31\frac{1}{2}$	32	$32\frac{1}{4}$
137	450	27	28	$28\frac{3}{4}$	$29\frac{1}{2}$	30	$30\frac{3}{4}$	$31\frac{1}{4}$	$31\frac{1}{4}$	32	$32\frac{1}{2}$	33	$33\frac{1}{4}$	$33\frac{3}{4}$

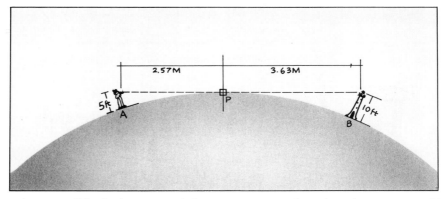

miles away. If both observers and the point P were in line, then observer A would just be able to see observer B, even though they were 6.2 miles apart!

ie 2.57 + 3.63 = 6.2 miles.

Distance Off

The distance off or range of lights either just rising above, or just dipping below the horizon can therefore be calculated by adding the individual dipping distances. Tables are available in which these additions for a range of observer and light heights are already done. Table 2 is an example of such a table and this is also taken from Reeds Almanac.

The use of these tables enable the range of a *defined light* to be determined with some certainty. It follows therefore that by taking a bearing on such a light at the time the range is established, a **fix** can be obtained.

Sectored Lights

The bearings of sectored lights are always measured from **seaward**. For example if the description of a light were given as:

R 090°–180°; G 180°–270°

it would have the following appearance:

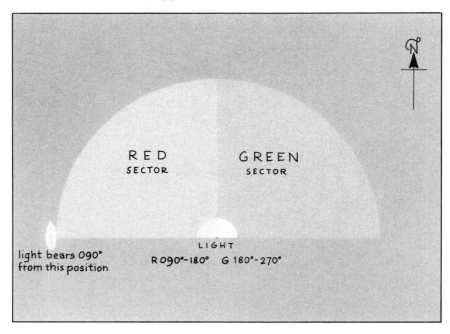

41

a An observer's height is 2.1 metres. What is the distance to his horizon?

b At what range will a buoy 8 feet high be visible to an observer over the horizon, 6 ft above the water level.

c What is the range of a light 91 ft above sea level from an observer 10 ft above sea level?

Answers to Chapter 5

Exercise 1

a Sunset to sunrise and as necessary during daylight hours.

b Dead ahead to 22.5° abaft the beam.

c A vessel towing.

d Port and starboard (can be combined) side lights and a stern light or; all-round red over an all-round green at the masthead together with a stern light.

Exercise 2

a 3.04 miles

b 6.06 miles

c 23.5 miles

Tides—depths, heights and rises

The important features of tides that affect navigation are:

- the depth of water
- the direction of flow, and
- the rate of flow

Tides are caused by the rise and fall of the surface of the sea which is in turn caused by the gravitational influence of the moon and the sun.

Lunar and Solar Tides

Lunar tides are caused by and the proximity of the moon exerting a gravitational pull on the earth and attracting the surface of the sea towards it. This results in an increase in the depth of water at those parts of the earth closest to the moon. Rotation of the earth causes the increase in depth to move around the earth from west to east. The effect is not instantanous, some delay occurs, about one and half days. This is due to the shape of the land masses and the size and shape of the sea.

Solar tides are similarly caused by the position of the sun, but the response in this instance is very much less and the delay or lag is greater.

Spring and Neap Tides

Spring tides are *not* annual events. They occur soon after each new and full moon, that is at about every fourteen days. When the moon and sun are aligned and on the same side of the earth (ie new moon) high spring tides occur. When they are aligned on opposite sides of the earth (full moon), the spring tides are lower. The orbit of the moon around the earth is elliptical and when the moon is farthest from the earth (ie in apogee) spring tides will be less than average.

Equinoctial springs occur at about the Equinoxes. That is when the periods of day and night are about equal (March 21st and September 23rd). At this time, spring tides are greater than average.

Neap tides occur when the moon and sun are in quadrature, ie when their pull is at right angles to each other. Similar conditions of lag to spring tides obtain.

Navigation

The marine navigator must be able to *predict* accurately the tidal movement in his area so that he can calculate with confidence the depth of water beneath his keel at any time.

Depths

The depth at any time is calculated by adding the known depth below a datum to the height of tide for that particular time of day and place. The depths are known as *soundings* and these are denoted on metric charts in metres and on some charts, fathoms and feet. A metric sounding shown as 15_5 indicates a depth *below* datum of 15.5 metres. On a **fathom** chart 15_5 denotes 15 fathoms 5 feet *not 15.5* fathoms. **Check your chart carefully!**

The datum is known as Chart Datum (CD) and this is a level based upon the

Lowest Astronomical Tide (LAT) at Newlyn. This has been adopted by international agreement as the standard for the UK. On fathom charts soundings are generally referred to *Mean Low Water Springs*. **Check carefully!**

The depths *above* CD vary from place to place and according to the state of the tide. The actual depths are calculated from values given in tide tables published by the Admiralty and in the leading almanacs (Reed's and Macmillan's).

To calculate the depth of water at a position at any specific time, one must determine, using the tables, the *height of tide* for that time and position and to add it to the sounding given on the chart for that position:

Sounding given	15.5 m
Height of tide	7.3 m
Depth of water	22.8 metres

Drying Heights

A drying height is the height of a feature *above* chart datum. On a chart this value or height is underlined.

eg $\underline{2_5}$ on a **metric chart** would indicate that that feature or area of the chart protrudes *above* the water 2.5 metres when the tide level is at chart datum. On **fathom charts** drying heights are normally given in *feet* (fractions of a foot are not used).

To determine the depth of water above such a feature it is necessary to *subtract* the drying height from the height of tide.

Height of tide	7.3 m
Sounding	2.5 m (Drying)
Depth of water	4.8 metres

We have already made reference to phrases such as chart datum, drying height and soundings. There are a number of standard phrases and expressions used in tidal work that it is important to know and understand. These are illustrated and defined below.

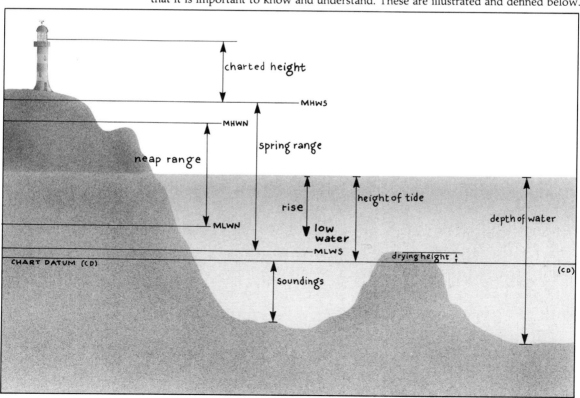

Tidal Definitions

Chart Datum. The level to which soundings and drying heights are referred on the chart and above which, heights of tide are given in the tide tables. The level of chart datum generally coincides with the level of lowest astronomical tide (LAT). This is the lowest level to which the tide can be expected to fall under average meteorological conditions and under any combination of astronomical conditions.

Mean High Water Springs (MHWS), Mean Low Water Springs (MLWS). These are the average heights of high and low water at spring tides. The charted heights of terrestrial objects (lights, peaks, bridges, etc) are referred to the level of Mean High Water Springs.

Mean High Water Neaps (MHWN), Mean Low Water Neaps (MLWN). These are the average heights of high and low water at neap tides.

Mean Tide Level. This is the average value of all the heights of high and low water over a period. This level does not always coincide with mean sea-level, but both terms are often referred to as mean level. Ordnance Datum (Newlyn) is the land reference level and corresponds to the average value of mean sea-level at Newlyn during 1915–21.

Height of Tide. The vertical distance between chart datum and the sea level.

Spring Range. The difference in height between MHWS and MLWS.

Neap Range. The difference in height between MHWN and MLWN.

Charted Sounding. The depth to the sea bed below chart datum.

Drying Height. The height above chart datum of features which are periodically covered and uncovered by the tides.

High Water (HW). The highest level reached by the tide in one tidal oscillation.

Low Water (LW). The lowest level reached by the tide in one tidal oscillation.

Range of the Tide. The vertical difference in height between successive high and low waters.

Duration of the Tide. The interval in time between successive high and low waters.

Interval from High Water. The interval in time between a given time and the nearest high water. Either − (before) or + (after) high-water time.

Rise. The vertical difference between the low water height and the water level.

Twelfths Rule

For a number of areas, those with a sinusoidal tidal curve, the twelfths rule enables depths of tide to be calculated with reasoable accuracy. In some areas however, the application of this rule would give rise to serious errors. The coastline between Portland and Selsey Bill is such an area.

The rule states that:

A tidal rise of 1/12 of the range occurs in the 1st hour after Low Water
A tidal rise of 2/12 of the range occurs in the 2nd hour after Low Water
A tidal rise of 3/12 of the range occurs in the 3rd hour after Low Water
A tidal rise of 3/12 of the range occurs in the 4th hour after Low Water
A tidal rise of 2/12 of the range occurs in the 5th hour after Low Water
A tidal rise of 1/12 of the range occurs in the 6th hour after Low Water

Thus at 2 hours after LW the total *rise* is $1/12 + 2/12 = 3/12$. ie 1/4 of the range.

When accuracy is essential the spring and neap tidal curves should be used. These are given in Admiralty tide tables and nautical almanacs for standard ports, together with times and heights of high and low water.

Tidal Calculations and Time Zones

Make sure that you are using the correct table!

Carry out all calculations in GMT; less chance of error will arise and the answer can be converted to BST if necessary, by finally adding 1 hour.

Information for French Atlantic and Channel ports is referred to as Time Zone − 1.00. To convert these times to GMT you must *subtract* one hour.

ie If High water Dieppe is 1400 (time zone − 1.00)
   High water Dieppe = 1300 GMT.

Exercise 1

Using the rule of twelfths and the following tide table extracts:

Time Zone GMT	Time	m	Time Zone −0100	Time	m
DOVER June 26	0516	5.7	Le HAVRE July 29	0324	1.7
Friday	1214	1.7	Wed	0909	7.2
	1742	5.9		1558	1.6
				2139	7.4

What is the rise of tide:
a 2 hours after low water when the range is 9 m?
b 5 hours after LW when the range is 6 m?
c What is the height of tide at Dover at 1414 GMT on June 26th?
d What is the height of tide at Le Havre at 1109 BST on July 29th?

Calculating Depths and Clearances

When calculating depths and clearances a diagram of the problem helps to clarify the arithmetic. The diagram should indicate the data and the requirement. The following example explains how.

Example

Problem

What rise is needed to give a clearance of 1 m, given drying height 2 m and draft 1.5 m.?

Step 1 List the data.   Drying height 2 m
                          Draft 1.5 m
                          Clearance 1 m

Step 2 Draw the diagram.

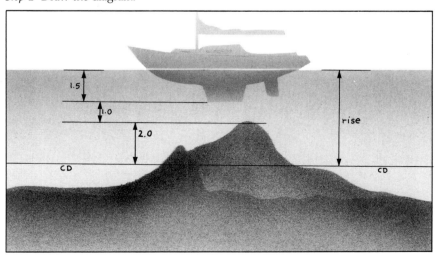

The rise needed = 1.5 + 1 + 2 = 4.5 m

47

a What depth of water will prevail when the charted depth is given as 2.5 m and the height of tide is 3.0 m?

b What would be the depth of water in a position where the charted depth is 3.9 m and the height of tide is 2.7 m?

c What is the minimum height of tide that will allow a boat of 1.5 m draft to cross a shoal charted as drying 1.5m, with a clearance of 0.75 m?

d What is the minimum height of tide which will allow a yacht drawing 2 m to cross a bar charted as drying 0.8 m, with a clearance of 0.4 m?

e A yacht anchors in 5.1 m when the height of tide is 2.6 m. Next high water is predicted at 6.3 m. What will be the depth of water at high water?

f A yacht is anchored in a depth of 4.5 m. At the time of anchoring the height of tide is 1.9 m. The predicted height of the next tide is 4.9 m. What will be the depth of water on the anchorage at high water?

g The least depth of water recorded on an echo sounder on entering harbour was 4.5 m. The transducer is located 0.3 m below the waterline and the sounder is calibrated to read the depth below the transducer. If the least charted depth at the entrance is stated to be 1.5 m. What was the height of tide at the time the yacht entered the harbour?

h The least depth of water recorded on a yacht's echo sounder as she enters harbour is 3.1 m. The transducer is 0.8 m below the water line and the sounder is calibrated to read depth below the transducer. If the least charted depth in the entrance is 2.0 m. What was the height of tide when the yacht entered harbour?

Heights at standard ports

The tidal heights for specific **standard ports** (eg Dover, Portsmouth, Dieppe etc), given in the almanacs and tide tables are for high and low water. To determine the height of tide at any other time, the tidal curve is used. In order to use the curve it is first necessary to determine three values viz;

    a The height of high water

    b The height of low water

    c The time of high water

    A typical curve and the procedure for its use is given below:

a Mark the high and low water values from the tide tables, at the top and bottom of the chart. (Left hand side H & L)

b Draw a straight line to connect these two points.

c Enter the time of high water for the day in the box below the centre of the curve. (C)

d For the time selected (t), ie so many hours before or after high water, determine the intercept on the curve corresponding to that time. (Point D)

e Draw a horizontal line from D to intercept the sloping line drawn in b (point E).

f Read off from the intercept (E) the value of the height of tide, from either the top or bottom scale of values (point F).

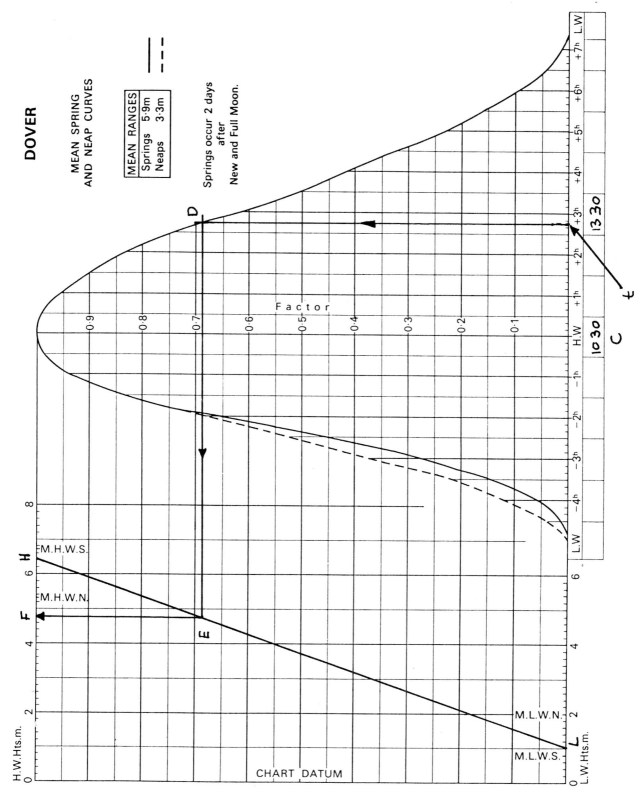

DOVER

MEAN SPRING
AND NEAP CURVES

MEAN RANGES	
Springs	5·9m
Neaps	3·3m

Springs occur 2 days
after
New and Full Moon.

49

(Use Dover tidal curve on page 49)
Time Zone GMT DOVER

	time	m		time	m
June 5	0031	6.7	July 4	0019	6.6
Fr	0811	0.6	Sa	0806	0.8
	1300	6.6		1243	6.6
	2027	0.7		2022	0.7
Aug 10	0046	2.2	Aug 18	0011	6.6
Mo	0650	5.1	Tu	0749	0.9
	1313	2.4		1235	6.8
	1917	5.3		2009	0.8

Using the tidal data above, what is the height of tide at Dover on:

a June 5th at 1830 BST?

b Aug 10th at 1150 BST?

At what time (BST) will a vessel drawing 1.5 m, clear by 0.5 m a sandbank at Dover awash at low tide on the morning of:

c Aug 18th?

d July 4th?

Heights at secondary ports

Secondary ports are places where the *heights* and *times* of high and low water differ from its standard port but where the *tidal flow* can be described by the tidal curve for the particular standard port. These *differences* are published and are used to calculate the times and heights of high and low water. They are presented in almanacs and tide tables however, in different forms. The manner in which they are used is best illustrated by applying the two systems to the same problem. Example 1 below, does this using the 'Reed's system' tidal data and Example 2 addresses the same problem using the 'Macmillan's system'.

Example 1

Using Reed's Data

Problem Use Reed's type tidal data to determine the depth of water at Calais at 1400 on July 7th.

The differences for Calais are based on Dunkerque. The tidal data for which are as follows:

Time Zone − 0100	h. min	m	Tidal Differences on DUNKERQUE				
				MHW		MLW	
Dunkerque July 7	0427	5.4		h. min	m	h. min	m
Tuesday	1124	0.9					
	1651	5.2	St Valery sur	− 035	+ 1.2	—	—
	2346	1.1	Somme				
			Calais	− 025	+ 1.0	− 020	+ 0.6

To solve the problem it is necessary to calculate three values to enable entry to the Dunkerque tidal curve, these are;

a The time of HW at Calais.

b The height of HW at Calais.

c The height of LW at Calais.

From the table for Dunkerque above:

Time of HW Calais	$= 1651 - 025 = 1626$
Height of HW Calais	$= 5.2 + 1.0 = 6.2$ m
Height of LW Calais	$= 0.9 + 0.6 = 1.5$ m

These values are entered on the Dunkerque tidal curve overleaf. The values for high

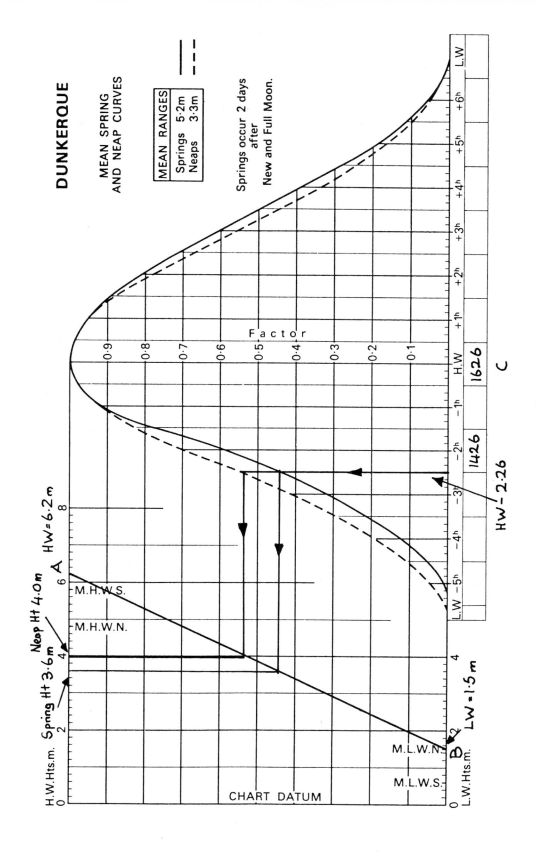

and low water have been entered at A and B and joined by a straight line. The time for high water has been entered at C and a line has been drawn vertically from the point on the baseline corresponding to 1400 hrs ie HW − 2.26. The intercept with the slanting straight line gives two depths when read off from along the top line. One from the spring curve of 3.6 m and the other from the neap curve of 4.0 m.

The range at Dunkerque on July 7th is 4.1 m ie 5.2 − 0.9. This is about halfway between the spring and neap ranges given on the curve and the height of tide will also be about halfway between 4.0 and 3.6 ie 3.8 m.

Exercise 4

(Use Dover tidal curve on page 49)

Tidal Differences on DOVER	MHW		MLW	
	h. min	m	h. min	m
Dungeness	− 015	+ 1.2	− 015	+ 0.2
Deal	+ 015	− 0.4	+ 005	0.0
Ramsgate	+ 020	− 1.6	− 007	− 0.6

Using the tidal differences above and tidal data given in Exercise 3, what is the height of tide at:

a Ramsgate on July 4th at 1100 BST?

b Dungeness on Aug 18th at 1725 BST?

Example 2

Using Macmillan's Data

Problem Use Macmillan's table of differences below to determine the depth of water at Calais at 1400 on July 7th.

Time Zone − 0100 DIEPPE

	h. min	m
July 7	0321	8.5
Tuesday	1007	1.4
	1542	8.0
	2228	1.7

Standard Port DIEPPE

Times					Height (metres)			
	HW		LW		MHWS	MHWN	MLWN	MLWS
	0100	0600	0700	0000	9.3	7.2	2.5	0.6
	1300	1800	1900	1200				
Differences CALAIS								
	+ 0043	+ 0057	+ 0054	+ 0105	− 2.1	− 1.2	− 0.3	+ 0.3

Consider the first two columns of the 'difference table' immediately above. The differences for HW Calais are given as + 0043 and + 0057. These relate to the times of HW at the standard port, Dieppe, given immediately above.

ie when HW Dieppe occurs at 0100 or 1300, HW Calais is 43 mins later
and when HW Dieppe occurs at 0600 or 1800, HW Calais is 57 mins later.

Now consider columns 5 & 6, these show that when;
HW Dieppe = 9.3   HW Calais = 9.3 − 2.1 = 7.2 m
and when HW Dieppe = 7.2   HW Calais = 7.2 − 1.2 = 6.0 m

Now consider columns 7 & 8, these show that when;
LW Dieppe = 2.5   LW Calais = 2.5 − 0.3 = 2.2 m
and when LW Dieppe = 0.6   LW Calais = 0.6 + 0.3 = 0.9 m

On July 7th, the day in question, HW Dieppe occurs at 1542. HW Calais will therefore occur sometime between 43 and 57 minutes later (cols 1 & 2).

Furthermore HW on that day is 8.0 m, ie between MHWS (9.3) and MHWN (7.2). The differences will thus also be between −2.1 and −1.2 (cols 5 & 6).

Finally, LW for the day is 1.4 m and this lies between MLWN and MLWS (cols 7 & 8).

It is necessary to calculate the three values required to enable entry to the Dieppe tidal curve, namely:

a The time of HW at Calais.

b The height of HW at Calais.

c The height of LW at Calais.

There are various ways to determine the intermediate differences arising from the values given by the Macmillan's system.

    i A simple *approximation* can be used.

    ii A *graph* can be drawn.

or **iii** They can be determined by *calculation*.

Method 1 Approximation

Time of HW

    From the 'difference table' we can see that: :

        at 1300 the difference is + 43 mins

    and at 1800 the difference is + 57 mins

1542 (time of HW of the day) is just over halfway between 1300 and 1800 and the difference therefore will be about halfway between 43 and 57 mins.

$$\text{ie} \quad \frac{43 + 57}{2}$$
$$= \frac{100}{2}$$
$$= 50 \, \text{mins}$$

Therefore HW Calais = 1542 + 50 mins = 1632

Height of HW

It can be seen that 8 m (ht of the day) lies about halfway between the Spring height 9.3 m and the Neap height 7.2 m (Difference table). The difference must therefore be about halfway between −2.1 and −1.2.

Ignore the minus sign for a while and calculate the midway value which is equal to.

$$\frac{2.1 + 1.2}{2}$$
$$= \frac{3.3}{2}$$
$$= 1.65 \quad \text{Now restore the minus sign and the difference is:}$$

Difference = − 1.65

We know however that 8 m was not quite halfway between the two high water values so we could legitimately reduce the value calculated to − 1.6 to allow for this.

∴ HW Calais = HW Dieppe + difference
               = 8.0−1.6 (NB the difference is negative)
               = 6.4 m

Height of LW

It can be seen from the 'difference table' that LW of the day 1.4 m is almost equal to the midway value (1.55) between the spring height 2.5 m and the Neap height 0.6 m. The midway value of the differences is zero and this value can be assumed for a LW of 1.4 m.

$$\therefore \text{ HW Calais} = \text{HW Dieppe} + 0$$
$$= 1.4 \text{ m}$$

We now have the three required values for the tidal curve.

a The time of HW at Calais $= 1632$

b The height of HW at Calais $= 6.4$ m

c The height of LW at Calais $= 1.4$ m

These values have been entered on the Dieppe tidal curve. The height of tide at 1400 hrs (HW $- 2.32$) obtained is 4.4 m.

$\therefore$ Depth at Calais on July 7 at 1400 $= 4.4$ m

Exercise 5

(Use Dieppe tidal curve on page 55)

Time Zone −0100	h. min	m
Dieppe June 6	0211	9.1
Sat	0901	0.9
	1434	8.7
	2122	1.2

Standard Port DIEPPE

Times				Height (metres)			
HW		LW		MHWS	MHWN	MLWN	MLWS
0100	0600	0700	0000	9.3	7.2	2.5	0.6
1300	1800	1900	1200				
Differences Boulogne •							
+0015	+0026	+0036	+0037	+0.4	0.0	+0.3	+0.4
Differences St Valery sur Somme							
+0028	+0040		No data	+0.7	+0.8	No data	

Use the 'approximation' method and the tidal data above.

a What at Boulogne on June 6th is:
  i the time (BST) of the second high water?
  ii the height of the second HW?
  iii the height of the first LW?

b At what time can a vessel drawing 2 m, leave Boulogne with a clearance of 0.5 m on June 6th? Assume lock gates open at 0900 local time.

Method 2 Graphically

The same problem which, together with the tidal information is reproduced for convenience below, can also be solved graphically.

This entails drawing simple graphs of:

a HW times   vs   HW differences for the secondary port.
b MHW heights   vs   HW height differences.
c MLW heights   vs   LW height differences.

having plotted the graphs the differences can then be read for a range of tidal heights and times for the particular ports.

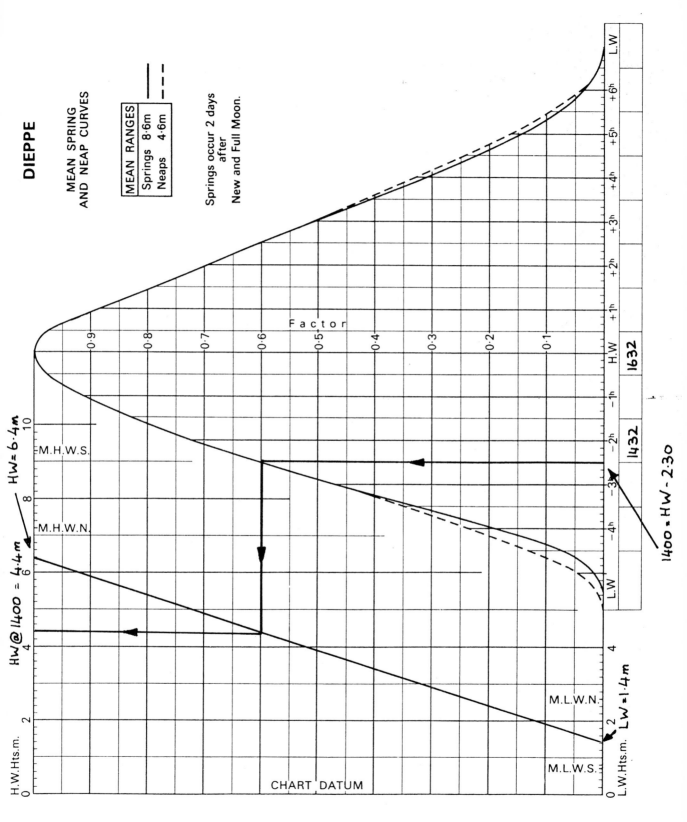

DIEPPE

MEAN SPRING
AND NEAP CURVES

MEAN RANGES
Springs 8·6m
Neaps 4·6m

Springs occur 2 days
after
New and Full Moon.

Factor

0·9
0·8
0·7
0·6
0·5
0·4
0·3
0·2
0·1

+6h +5h +4h +3h +2h +1h H.W. −1h −2h −3h −4h L.W.

1632
1432
1400 = HW − 2·30

HW = 6·4m
HW @ 1400 = 4·4m

M.H.W.S.
M.H.W.N.

LW = 1·4m

M.L.W.N.
M.L.W.S.

H.W.Hts.m.
L.W.Hts.m.

CHART DATUM

10
8
6
4
2
0

4
2
0

55

Problem Use Macmillan's type tidal data to determine the depth of water at Calais at 1400 on July 7th.

Time Zone − 0100	h. min	m
Dieppe July 7	0321	8.5
Tuesday	1007	1.4
	1542	8.0
	2228	1.7

Standard Port DIEPPE

Times					Height (metres)			
HW		LW			MHWS	MHWN	MLWN	MLWS
0100	0600	0700	0000		9.3	7.2	2.5	0.6
1300	1800	1900	1200					
Differences CALAIS								
+ 0043	+ 0057	+ 0054	+ 0105		− 2.1	− 1.2	− 0.3	+ 0.3

Time of HW
From the difference table,

	the HW times are:	0100	0600	1300	1800
	and the differences are:	+ 43	+ 57	+ 43	+ 57

Plot the values as shown below and read off the difference for a high water time of 1542 (HW of the day)

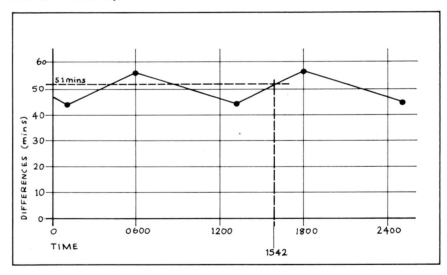

From the graph the difference at 1542 is seen to be 51 mins

$$\therefore \text{HW Calais} = 1542 + 0051 = 1633$$

Height of HW
Now plot the HW heights against the HW differences and read off the difference value for HW = 8.0 m.

Values: HW heights at Dieppe: 9.3   7.2
          HW differences at Calais: − 2.1   − 1.2

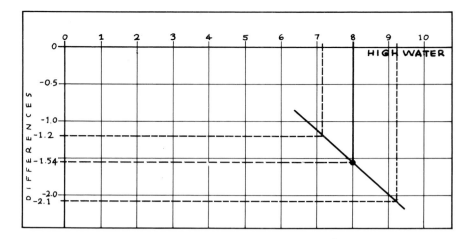

From the graph the difference for a height of 8.0 m is -1.54 m.

HW Calais = HW Dieppe − Differences

∴ HW Calais = 8.0 − 1.54

$= 6.46$

$= 6.5$ m approx

Height of LW

Now plot the LW heights against the LW differences and read off the difference value for LW = 1.4 m.

Values.

LW levels at Dieppe:	2.5	0.6
LW differences at Calais:	−0.3	+0.3

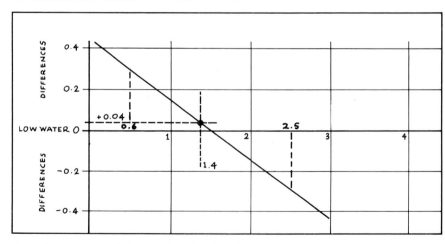

From the graph the difference for a height of 1.4 m is 0.04.

This can be ignored.

∴ LW Calais = LW Dieppe − difference

$= 1.4\,m − 0$

LW Calais = 1.4 m

We have now graphically determined the three required values for the tidal curve.

a The time of HW at Calais $= 1633$

b The height of HW at Calais $= 6.5$ m

c The height of LW at Calais $= 1.4$ m

Normally these values would be entered on the Dieppe tidal curve and a height of tide at 1400 determined. The values however are so similar to those obtained by method 1 that we can assume that the height at Calais at 1400 will again be 4.4 m.

A big advantage of using graphs is that they can be prepared in advance and that the difference *for any time or height* can be easily read off.

Exercise 6

(A Dieppe tidal curve for this exercise is provided on page 55)

Time zone −0100	h. min	m
Dieppe Aug 10	0111	2.8
Tuesday	0659	6.8
	1350	2.8
	1937	6.8

Standard Port DIEPPE

Times				Height (metres)			
HW		LW		MHWS	MHWN	MLWN	MLWS
0100	0600	0700	0000	9.3	7.2	2.5	0.6
1300	1800	1900	1200				
Differences Boulogne							
+0015	+0026	+0036	+0037	+0.4	0.0	+0.3	+0.4
Differences St Valery sur Somme							
+0028	+0040	No data		+0.7	+0.8	No data	

Using the graphic method and the tidal data above.
a What, at St Valery sur Somme on Aug 10th is:
  i the time (BST) of the *second* high water?
  ii the height of HW?
  iii the height of LW?
b At what time in the afternoon of Aug 10th, is the height of tide 4 m?

Method 3 Calculation
We will now address the self-same problem, reproduced again for convenience, and obtain a solution by calculation.

Problem – Use Macmillan's type tidal data to determine the depth of water at Calais at 1400 on July 7th.

Time Zone − 0100	h. min	m
Dieppe July 7	0321	8.5
Tuesday	1007	1.4
	1542	8.0
	2228	1.7

Standard Port DIEPPE

Times				Height (metres)			
HW		LW		MHWS	MHWN	MLWN	MLWS
0100	0600	0700	0000	9.3	7.2	2.5	0.6
1300	1800	1900	1200				
Differences CALAIS							
+0043	+0057	+0054	+0105	−2.1	−1.2	−0.3	+0.3

Time of HW
We require to determine the difference in time of HW at Calais when HW Dieppe is 1542. We can see that the differences increase from 43 mins at 1300 to 57 mins at

1800, an increase of 2.8 mins/hr. This value is calculated as follows;

The difference @ 1800	is	$+57$ mins	
and at 1300	is	$+43$ mins	$-$ (Subtract the values)

$$\text{5 hrs} \qquad \text{14 mins}$$

The differences in 5 hrs are thus 14 mins.

$$\therefore \text{ difference/hr} = \frac{14}{5} = 2.8 \text{ mins/hr}$$

We now need to determine the difference at 1542.

From the table the difference at 1300 is $+0043$, and 1542 is 2 hrs 42 mins (2.7 hrs) later than 1300.

$$\therefore \text{Differences at } 1542 = \text{differences at } 1300 + (2.7 \times \text{the difference/hr})$$
$$= 43 + (2.7 \times 2.8)$$
$$= 43 + 7.56$$
$$= 50.56 \text{ mins (51 mins approx)}$$

$$\therefore \text{ HW Calais on July 7th} = 1542 + 0051 = 1633$$

Height of HW

The heights and differences are given in columns 5 & 6 of the table above. The height at Calais is calculated using similar methods as were used to calculate the *time* differences.

By subtracting MHWN (col 6) from MHWS (col 5) the range of *mean high water* MHW is obtained. Similarly by subtracting the differences a *range of differences* is obtained. The table below gives the HW heights and differences together with the ranges of MHW and differences.

	MHWS	MHWN	
Height (metres)	9.3	7.2	Range of MHW $= 9.3 - 7.2 = 2.1$m
Differences	-2.1	-1.2	Range of Diffs $= 2.1 - 1.2 = 0.9$ m

We need to determine the *height difference* at Calais when HW Dieppe $= 8.0$ m. It will be somewhere between -2.1 and -1.2.

The *height difference* at Calais can be calculated using the following formula;

$$\text{Difference} = \text{diff @ MHWN} + \left\{ \frac{(\text{HW of day}) - \text{MHWN}}{\text{Range of MHW}} \times (\text{range of differences}) \right\}$$

NB If HW of the day is less than MHWN use

$$\text{Difference} = \text{diff @ MHWN} + \left\{ \frac{\text{MHWN} - (\text{HW of day})}{\text{Range of MHW}} \times (\text{range of differences}) \right\}$$

Ignore the minus sign for the differences for a while

$$\text{Difference} = 1.2 + \left\{ \frac{(8 - 7.2)}{2.1} \times 0.9 \right\}$$
$$= 1.2 + .34$$
$$= 1.54 \quad \text{now restore the minus sign}$$
$$\text{Difference} = -1.54$$

$$\therefore \text{ HW Calais} = \text{HW Dieppe} + \text{difference}$$
$$= 8.0 - 1.54$$
$$= 6.46 \text{ m}$$
$$\text{HW Calais} = 6.5 \text{ m approx}$$

Height of LW

The height of low water at Calais is calculated using similar methods as were used to calculate the high water value.

By subtracting MLWS (col 8) from MLWN (col 7) the range *mean low water* MLW is obtained. Similarly by subtracting the differences ie subtracting the lowest value from the highest, a *range of differences* is obtained. The table below gives the LW heights and differences together with the ranges of MLW and Differences.

	MLWN	MLWS	
Height (metres)	2.5	0.6	Range of MLW $= 2.5 - 0.6 = 1.9$
Differences	-0.3	$+0.3$	Range of Differences $= 0.3 - (-0.3) = 0.6$

We need to determine the *height difference* at Calais when LW Dieppe is 1.4m. The *Magnitude* of this value can be calculated using the following formula;

$$\text{Difference} = \text{diff @ MLWS} \pm \left\{ \frac{(\text{LW of day}) - \text{MLWS}}{\text{Range of MLW}} \times \begin{array}{l}(\text{range of}\\ \text{differences})\end{array} \right\}$$

NB If LW of the day is less than MLWS use

$$\text{Difference} = \text{diff @ MLWS} \pm \left\{ \frac{\text{MLWS} - (\text{LW of day})}{\text{Range of MLW}} \times \begin{array}{l}(\text{range of}\\ \text{differences})\end{array} \right\}$$

$$\text{Difference} = 0.3 \pm \left\{ \frac{(1.4 - 0.6)}{1.9} \times 0.6 \right\}$$

$= 0.3 \pm 0.25$ by inspection the sign is obviously negative as the difference must lie between -0.3 and $+0.3$.

$\therefore$ Difference $= 0.3 - 0.25$

$= 0.05$

$\therefore$ LW Calais $=$ LW Dieppe $+$ Difference

$= 1.4 + 0.05$

$= 1.45$ m.

We have now calculated the three values for the Tidal curve.

a The time of HW at Calais $= 1633$

b The height of HW at Calais $= 6.46$ m

c The height of LW at Calais$= 1.45$ m

These values again would be entered on the curve but as a similar result has been obtained this will not be necessary.

Let us now compare the results for the three methods.

		Method 1 Approx'n	Method 2 Graphs	Method 3 Calcul'n
a	The time of HW at Calais	$= 1632$	1633	1633
b	The height of HW Calais	$= 6.4$ m	6.46 m	6.46 m
c	The height of LW Calais	$= 1.4$ m	1.4 m	1.45 m

The spread of results using the three methods is small, 1 minute in time and 0.05 m (less than 2 inches) in height. It is therefore a matter of personal preference as to which to use. What is important to note is that the three methods used are *mathematical treatments* of the problem. The object of the lesson was to demonstrate how the calculations are performed. In practice, tides are considerably influenced by wind strength and direction and *allowance based upon experience must be made for this*. Calculations for tidal heights and times implying accuracies to within minutes and centimetres, are a nonsense. Figures must be rounded up to give an adequate margin of safety.

(A DOVER tidal curve is provided on page 49)

Time Zone GMT DOVER

	h. min	m
June 5	0031	6.7
Fr	0811	0.6
	1300	6.6
	2027	0.7

Standard Port DOVER

Times				*Height (metres)*			
HW		*LW*		*MHWS*	*MHWN*	*MLWN*	*MLWS*
0000	0600	0100	0700	6.7	5.3	2.0	0.8
1200	1800	1300	1900				
Differences Deal							
+0010	+0020	+0010	+0005	−0.6	−0.3	0.0	0.0

Using the calculation method and the tidal data above.

a What, at Deal on June 5th is:

   i the time (BST) of the second high water?

   ii the height of HW?

   iii the height of LW?

b At what time in the morning of June 5th, is the height of tide 2m?

Clearances below bridges

There remains one further aspect of tidal levels that affects safe navigation and that is the determination of the clearance below bridges. The clearance will vary with the state of the tide and this therefore is an important part of the calculation.

The problem entails establishing accurately the clearance between the water level, at any specific time, and the underside of the bridge and then to determine whether there is sufficient clearance to enable the vessel to pass safely beneath.

The stated clearance below a bridge is measured from the height of mean high water springs, (MHWS) to the underside of the bridge. Values for MHWS can be found in some almanacs for the port in question but otherwise they are given on the charts for the area.

Consider the following problem. A yacht's truck (masthead) is 10m above the waterline. She wishes to pass beneath a bridge charted as 9 m. MHWS for the area is 4.7 m. What is the maximum height of tide which will enable the vessel to pass safely beneath the bridge for a clearance of 0.5 m?

First illustrate the problem with a simple diagram.

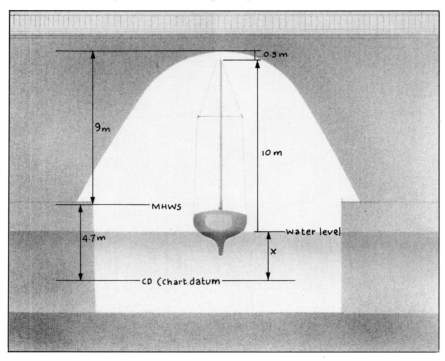

The height of the mast is 10 m and the required clearance is 0.5 m.
The overall clearance required is therefore $10 + 0.5 = 10.5$ m
The charted height of the bridge is given as 9 m
and MHWS for the area is 4.7 m
The height of the underside of the bridge above CD is then
$$9 + 4.7 = 13.7 \text{ m}$$
Let x = the maximum height of the tide
Then $x = 13.7 - 10.5$
$\therefore x = 3.2$ m

(A Dover tidal curve for this exercise is provided at the end of the chapter)

Time Zone GMT	Time	m
Dover July 17	0614	1.1
Friday	1109	6.3
	1836	1.1
	2319	6.3

a A yacht's masthead is 11 m above the waterline. MHWS = 6.6 m, HW = 1100 6.4 m, LW = 0500 2.8 m. What is the latest time in the morning that she can clear a bridge charted as 8.6 m, with a clearance of 0.5 m? Use the rule of twelfths.

b What is the earliest time during daylight hours on Friday 17 July, that a yacht drawing 1.7 m, can leave a dock in Dover with a clearance of 0.3 m, when the cill is charted as drying 1 m? Use tidal data above.

Answers to Chapter 6

Exercise 1
a 2.25 m **b** 5.5 m **c** Range = 4.2 $\frac{1}{4}$ range = 1.05 Ht = 1.05 + 1.7 = 2.75 m
d Range = 5.6 $\frac{1}{4}$ range = 1.4 Ht = 7.2 − 1.4 = 5.8 m

Exercise 2
a 5.5 m **b** 6.6 m **c** 3.75 m **d** 3.2 m **e** 8.8 m **f** 7.5 m **g** 4.8 − 1.5 = 3.3 m
h 1.9 m

Exercise 3
a 2.6 m **b** 3.5 m **c** 1050 BST (spring curve) **d** 1100 BST

Exercise 4
a 1.8 m **b** 6.7 m

Exercise 5
a i 1452 BST **ii** 9.0 m (approx $\frac{2}{3}$ springs) **iii** 1.3 m (diff = + 0.35)
b 10.37 (Local time) (HW − 4.15 ($\frac{2}{3}$ springs))

Exercise 6
a i 2014 BST **ii** 7.6 m **iii** 2.8 m (No data for St V-s-S, use LW Dieppe)
b HW − 0355 = 1619 BST (Range = 4.82 m ∴ use Neap curve)

Exercise 7
a i 1412 BST (1312 GMT) **ii** 6.0 (diff = − 0.58) **iii** 0.6 m (diff = 0)
b 1002 GMT 1102 BST

Exercise 8
a 2 hrs after low water, ie 0700.
b 0929 BST (HW − 2.40)

Buoyage

Buoys are provided and used to enable safe navigation in hazardous areas. The 'direction of buoyage' is marked on Admiralty charts with a large open arrow and two dots, thus:

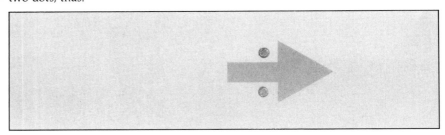

This indicates the direction of the flood tide and in the *direction shown*, **port-hand** buoys are to be left to port (on the left) and **starboard-hand** buoys are to be left to starboard (on the right). This might seem perfectly obvious but it is **most important** to get it right. The direction of buoyage in UK waters and most European waters is such that when **entering** a port or harbour, **port** hand markers are left to **port** ie to your left. (In the USA they do it the other way round). It follows therefore that when **leaving** harbour, because you will then be travelling against the direction of buoyage, port hand markers must be left to starboard side (on the right). Hence the need fully to understand *direction of buoyage.*

Lateral marks

Port-Hand Buoys   These are of various shapes and generally are flat topped or have a flat topped pinnacle. They are coloured **red** and when lit, carry red lights. They are also known as red can buoys. Lights: red, any rhythm.

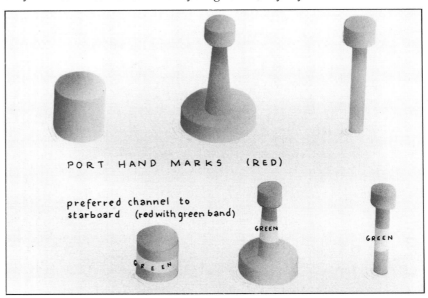

PORT HAND MARKS   (RED)

preferred channel to
starboard   (red with green band)

GREEN

GREEN

GREEN

Starboard-Hand Buoys These are also of various shapes but in general are conical and have cone shaped pinnacles. They are coloured **green** and carry green lights when lit. Lights: green, any rhythm.

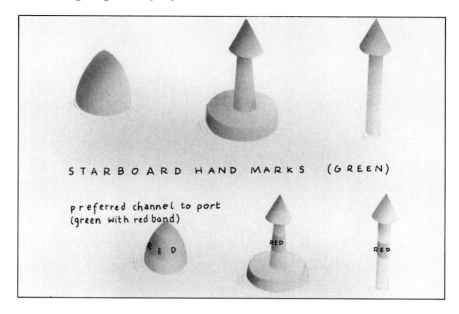

Cardinal Marks These are pillar type buoys, coloured black and yellow, in bands. They are surmounted by **two black cones**. There are four different types, one for each of the four compass cardinal points. They differ from lateral marks in one important respect. Safe water for a cardinal mark, say a *north cardinal mark*, lies to the **north** of that buoy. A Lateral mark, say a *starboard*-hand buoy is safely *left to starboard*, when travelling in the direction of buoyage. This principle is illustrated below.

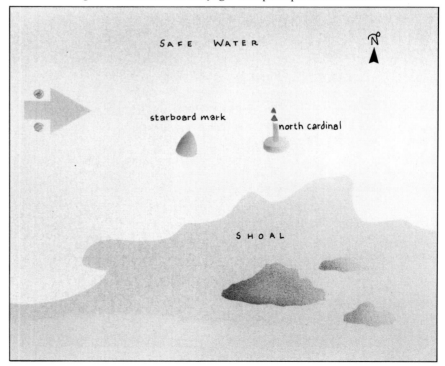

The *cardinal marks* have distinctive double top cones and the direction in which these point, indicate the type and the position of the black bands on the black and yellow banded body of the buoy, eg, on a west cardinal buoy the points of the cones are together and the centre band, on the buoy itself, is black. They are also uniquely identified by flashing light codes. They are illustrated below, together with the manner in which they are deployed to mark a hazardous area.

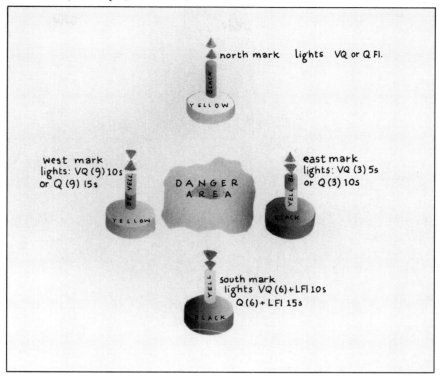

Bifurcation or Modified Lateral Marks   These are used to mark where a channel divides and where either branch can be navigated. The marks are either:

a A **red** can buoy with a **green** centre band, indicating, preferred channel to the *right*, ie leave the mark to *port*.
Lights: group flashing, eg Fl (2 + 1) R.

b A **green** conical buoy with a **red** centre band, indicating, preferred channel to the *left* ie leave the mark to *starboard*.
Lights: group flashing, eg Fl (2 + 1) G.

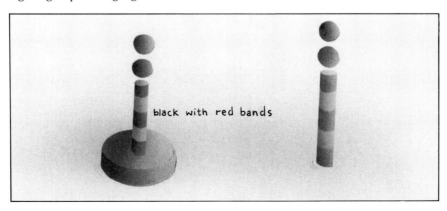

Isolated Danger Marks   These are pillar or spar buoys coloured **red** and **black** in horizontal bands. The buoy is surmounted by **two black spheres** mounted one above the other. Lights: white Gp Fl (2). See illustration on page 67.

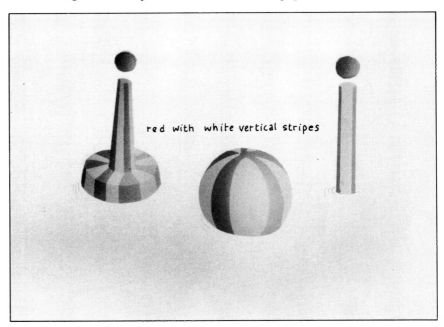

red with white vertical stripes

Safe Water Marks   These are sometimes referred to as fairway buoys. They are coloured **red** and **white** in vertical stripes. They vary in shape and size and are mainly either spherical, spar or pillar buoys. They are surmounted by **one red ball**. Lights: white, isophase, occulting, one long flash (10 secs), or Morse A (· −)

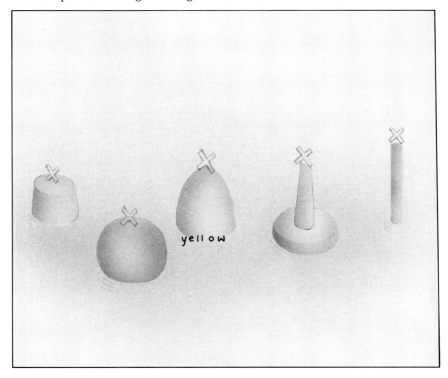

yellow

Special Marks These can be any of the shapes above and are used to mark spoil grounds, recreation zones, or as racing marks. They are coloured **yellow** and usually have an **X top mark**. Lights: yellow. Rhythm: any, other than those prescribed for cardinal, isolated danger and or safe water marks. See page 68.

See page 68.

<table>
</table>

Exercise 1

a Describe the shape, colour and light characteristics of;
i An isolated danger mark.
ii A south cardinal buoy.
iii A starboard lateral mark.
iv A safe water mark.
b To which side should the following buoys or marks be left or passed?
i Port hand mark when leaving harbour.
ii North cardinal mark.
iii Isolated danger mark.
c What type of buoys have the following light characteristics?
i VQ (3) 5s
ii Gp fl (2)
iii R (3) 10s
d What type of buoys have the following top marks?
i Two black cones, points uppermost?
ii One red sphere?
iii A yellow cross?

Answers to Chapter 7

a
i Spar or pillar buoy; red and black bands surmounted by two black spheres, one above the other. Lights: Gp fl (2) white.
ii Pillar buoy, yellow top half and black base. Surmounted by two black cones points down and one above the other. Lights: quick or very quick flash (6 + 1 long flash).
iii Conical or spar with conical top mark, coloured green. Lights: green, any rhythm.
iv Spherical, spar or pillar, red and white vertical stripes; surmounted by one red sphere. Lights: isophase, occulting, one long flash or morse A white.
b
i Left to starboard.
ii Pass on the north side.
iii Pass either side but, keep well clear.
c
i East cardinal mark.
ii Isolated danger mark.
iii Port lateral mark.
d
i North cardinal mark.
ii Safe water mark or fairway buoy.
iii Special mark.

Effects of wind and tide in chartwork

In setting a direct course between two points, two elements (apart from compass errors) can influence or affect that course. These are the **wind** and the **tide**. It is therefore most necessary to have a good understanding of the effect of these elements and to be able to make due allowance for them when calculating a vessel's position.

Wind Effect (Leeway)

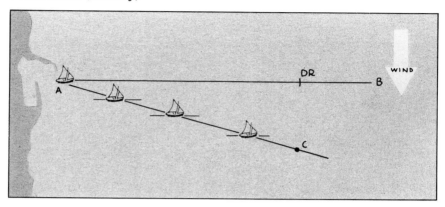

Consider the diagram above. The vessel's heading, or course, (ie the way the boat is pointing), is along the line AB. If nothing were to affect that course, the vessel would eventually arrive at position DR. This would be the dead reckoning (DR) position. The wind however is on the port beam and the vessel is blown off-course to some extent and in fact moves along the line AC. She does this even though she at all times is still heading (or pointing) in a direction parallel to the line AB. The line AC is thus the track that the vessel has made across the *water surface* and the vessel's wake would indeed have followed that line. The line AC is therefore known as the **wake course** or **water track**. The angle that AC makes with AB is known as the **leeway angle**. Unless proper allowance is made for this effect on a long voyage, a considerable error in your estimated position can result.

The leeway angle can be estimated by comparing the offset of the vessel's wake to her heading, or it can be measured by taking a back bearing (over the stern) of the vessel's wake course and subtracting the value obtained from the reciprocal of the boats **magnetic** (ie compass corrected for deviation) heading.

Exercise 1

Use the Stanford Channel Islands Chart.
a A vessel is sailing from the NW Minquiers buoy to St Martin's Point LH (Guernsey). The wind is NE and she is making 10° leeway. What is the *true* course she must steer? Ignore tidal effects. Var'n 5°W. Dev'n 0°.
b During the same voyage a bearing taken on Grosnez Point (Jersey) is 045°T and on La Corbière LH 090°T. The wind has backed to due-west. Leeway still 10°. What course must she now steer? Ignore tidal effects. Var'n 5°W Dev'n 0°.

Tidal Stream Effects

The tidal stream is the movement of water over the seabed. Its effect is to carry everything adrift, with it. It has exactly the same influence on a large liner as it does on a small yacht. The effect on the latter however is more noticable because of the yacht's lower speed.

Tidal streams flow more strongly at springs and less so at neaps. Around the British Isles an average rate of 1–3 knots is to be expected, but in races, rates as high as 6–7 knots can be encountered.

A race is caused by the interaction of a protruding headland on a fast moving tide stream, or where the tide stream flows quickly over shoaling areas.

Tides also affect sea conditions. When the tide is running against the wind, (wind over tide) the waves can become steep and short, quite high seas can be experienced in sheltered waters under these conditions and seas of 6–7 feet can be observed off Calshot in a Force 5.

Tides are also affected by coastline contours and tide streams invariably set into bays. Allowance for this should be made when sailing between headlands, particularly in bad visibility.

Tidal streams cannot be ignored by a yachtsman. It is difficult, sometimes impossible, to 'buck the tide' (sail against it). On the other hand, by timing your departure carefully to obtain maximum assistance from the tide, your effective ground speed can be increased considerably.

The direction and rate (speed) of the tides are given on most charts for each hour of the tide. On some charts this information is given in insert diagrams. On Admiralty charts it is given in the form of a table which is referred to about 8 or 12 specific positions on the chart identified thus: ◈ . These are known as the *tidal diamonds*. The table is itself referred to a standard port for tidal height information. When using a chart look carefully to ensure that you refer to the tidal information for the *correct* standard port. A typical extract from an Admiralty chart is given below:

Tidal Stream referred to St HELIER
◈ 49° 35.6'N
   2° 03.5'W

		Dirn	Rate Sp	Kn Np
Hours before HW	6	220°	5.4	2.5
	5	216°	5.3	2.5
	4	214°	4.3	2.0
	3	206°	2.2	1.0
	2	109°	0.7	0.3
	1	041°	3.5	1.6
	HW	032°	5.6	2.6
Hours after HW	1	030°	5.3	2.5
	2	031°	4.3	2.0
	3	033°	2.3	1.0
	4	114°	0.3	1.0
	5	221°	2.9	1.3
	6	221°	5.0	2.4

The above table shows that at 3 hrs before high water St Helier, the *direction* of the tide at ◈ is 206T and that its *rate* at springs is 2.2 kts; at neaps it is 1.0 kts. It is important to note that these rates and direction prevail for *half an hour each side* of the stated hour, ie from HW − 3.5 until HW − 2.5. The latitude and longitude of the position of each tidal diamond on the chart is also given.

The Admiralty also publish, for specific areas, a number of *Tidal Stream Atlases*.

These are in booklet form and give more detailed information than the charts. The tidal rates in these atlases are given for springs and neaps in *tenths of a knot*, eg 15 05 indicates a rate at springs of 1.5 kts and at neaps of 0.5 Kts.

Tidal Effects on Chartwork

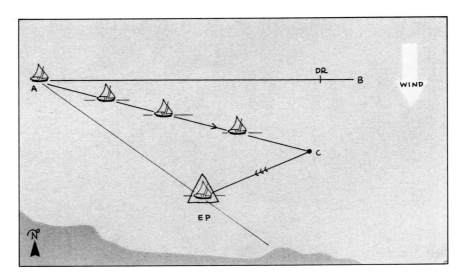

Consider the diagram above. We have already established that the wind would deflect us from our DR position and that if a heading of AB were maintained, we would eventually arrive at C. Assume that the voyage was sailed at a steady 4 knots and that we arrived at C after 1 hour. The length of the line A-C could then be scaled to equal 4 nautical miles (knots). If also during that voyage the tide had been flowing in a south-westerly direction at a steady 2 knots, then our vessel and everything else adrift, would have been moved in a south-westerly direction for 2 miles.

If we now draw the effect of that movement as a vector in a SW direction from point C on our chart, and then scale its length to equal 2 miles, we arrive at an estimated position for our vessel at the point EP. This is known as the **EP** (*estimated position*) and is calculated by making due allowance for wind, tide and the vessel's speed.

The line A-EP is in point of fact the track that the vessel has followed across the seabed during her voyage. This line is known as the *ground track*.

The four vectors shown are those which are drawn on a chart to enable the course and position of a vessel to be plotted. They and the positions are individually and specifically marked so that confusion does not arise. This is particularly important when watches are in operation and navigators change over.

The standard markings used in chartwork are as follows: Note that times are appended to positions.

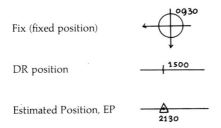

Fix (fixed position)

DR position

Estimated Position, EP

Ship's head, heading or course	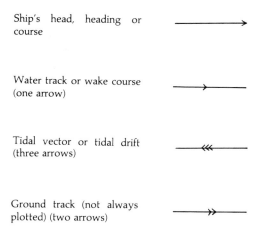
Water track or wake course (one arrow)	
Tidal vector or tidal drift (three arrows)	
Ground track (not always plotted) (two arrows)	

Their relationship, one to another is illustrated in the diagram below:

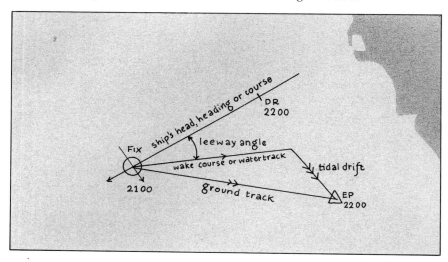

NB Speed made good or ground speed is the scaled distance travelled along the ground track vector in one hour.

Positions of Buoys and Light Vessels

The positions of buoys and light vessels are measured from the centre of the small circle drawn on the chart symbol at the base of the buoy or vessel. Abbreviations, By, LV and LH are frequently used to denote buoy, light vessel and lighthouse respectively.

Hourly Vectors

It is usual to plot courses by hourly vectors. This means that the plot is made up from the *water track* covered in one hour and the *tidal drift* for one hour, and hence an EP is determined.

Occasionally however it is more convenient to use half-hourly vectors and in some circumstances, to plot DR positions for several hours and then to offset for the tide at the end. It is to be noted that, whilst this latter plotting technique is simpler and suitable for solving class room problems, it is only safe in practice when navigating in *open water*.

a A vessel is sailing in poor visibility across a bay and between two headlands. The tide is dead astern. What precautions should she take in estimating her position and point of arrival?

b At 1300 a vessel is at position 49°45'N 2°03'W. She is heading 140° at 4 kts. The tide is setting 207°T at 6 kts

i What is her position at 1400?

ii What direction has she travelled across the ground?

iii What has been her ground speed?

c At 1500 a vessel is at 49°32'N 1°57'W and heading 258°T at 4 kts for St Peter Port. The tide is setting 153°T @ 1.5 kts from 1500–1600 and 180°T @ 2.0 kts from 1600–1700

What is her position at 1700?

d The same vessel maintains her course and speed for a further hour. If the tide has been setting 133T at 1.5 kts, what is the bearing and range of the Blanchard buoy (Sark) from her position at 1800?

e A vessel steers 230°M from the Blanchard buoy (Sark) at 5 kts. 1 hour later she is close by Banc Desormes buoy. What has been the direction and rate of the tide in that hour? Var'n 5°W Dev'n 0.

Running Fix with Tidal Stream and Leeway Effect

We have previously established how a position may be determined by taking two bearings on a fixed object, at two different times, and by maintaining and recording a steady course and speed between the two times. (Running fix.)

When your steady course is affected by the wind and tide, the same *basic* principles apply but, allowance has to be made for these extra effects.

Consider the following diagram.

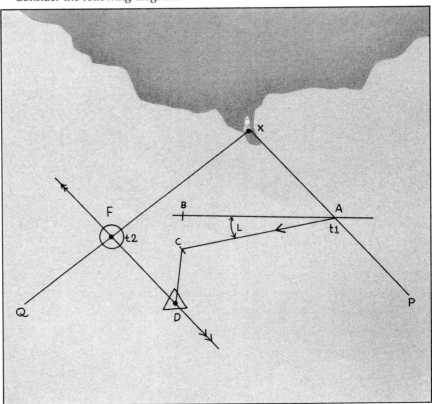

Bearings on X were taken at two different times, t1 and t2. The first indicated that our position was somewhere along the line XP. The second, along XQ. The problem is, to determine just where along XQ we are at time t2.

Our course is A-B and B is our DR position at time t2. The wind has blown us off-course and L is the resulting leeway angle. Allowing *only* for *wind* effects, we will now be at C at time t2. The tide for the period t1 to t2 has set us south-west and over a distance CD. Thus allowing for *wind* and *tide* our position is now at D and this position, because it allows for both winds and tide is an **EP**.

We know however that we are, at time t2, somewhere along line XQ. Transferring the bearing XP to a position such that it passes through the point D, will give an intercept of the bearing line XQ at point F. This is our true position at time t2 and is marked as a **fix**. The line FD is marked at each end with double arrows, these denote that that line is a transferred bearing.

Exercise 3

Use the Stanford Channel Islands chart.
a At 0900 a vessel on passage from St Brieuc to Sark, steering 039°C at a steady 5 knots, took a bearing on Grand Lejon LH of 105 M. At 1100 a further bearing of 210°M was taken on the same lighthouse. The tidal set and rate from 0900–1000 was 080°T at 3 kts and from 1000–1100 063°T at 2.2 kts. What was her position at 1100? Use variation 5 W and deviation 4 W.

b In question **a** above, what was the vessel's ground speed between 0900 and 1100?

Course setting

We are now able to plot a course from a known fixed position and to determine our final position after sailing some distance. This is fine, but what if our final position after sailing some distance is on a rock or sandbank? It is necessary therefore to not only be able to *PLOT* a course, but also to *SET* one: ie, to determine what course must be steered to get safely from A to B, allowing for wind and tide.

Setting a Course to Allow for Wind and Tide   The procedure is not too disimilar to *plotting* a course. The steps are simply taken in reverse order. Consider the diagram below.

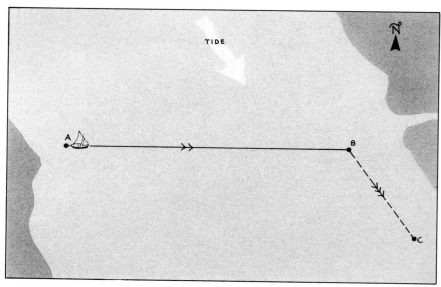

We wish to sail from A to B (ground track). If we set a direct course from A to B, the tide would, if setting SE as shown, cause our vessel to move so that we would eventually arrive at C. To arrive at B without constantly altering course, we must set a course which allows for the 'tidal set and rate' (direction and speed).

NB

A tide setting SE flows **to** the SE.

A SE wind however blows **from** the SE.

To determine the course to steer we first draw the ground track to our destination. Then set off the tidal vector from our fixed starting position.

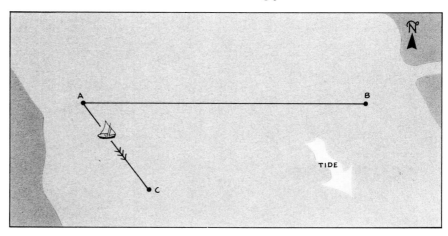

Assume the tidal rate was 1 knot. We then strike an arc of length equal to the scaled **planned** speed, say 2 knots, from C to cut the ground track (line AB).

NB

You **do not** join C to B.

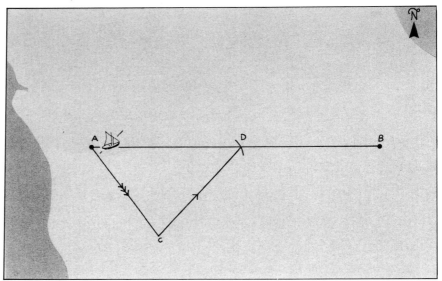

The bearing of the line CD is the *true* course to steer. It is the **wake** course and it is marked with one arrow. Its length is scaled to the vessel's speed (in this case 2 knots)

To obtain the **compass** course to steer, the **wake** course is adjusted to allow for variation and deviation. The course to steer is most dependent upon the vessel's speed. For different speeds, a different course will need to be set. This effect is illustrated below.

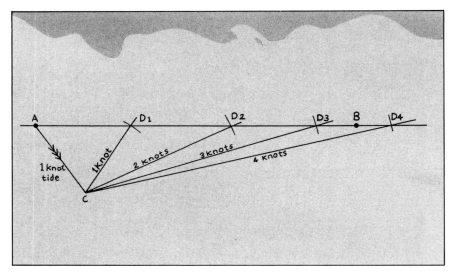

Summary

In summary therefore, to set a course it is necessary to carry out the following actions and in the order listed.

1 Draw the required *ground track.*

2 Plot the expected *tidal stream.*

3 Strike an arc from the tidal vector to cut the ground track. Measure its bearing; this is the *wake* course.

4 Apply correction for *leeway.*

5 Apply correction for *variation.*

6 Apply correction for *deviation.*

7 The result is the **compass** course to steer.

Exercise 4

Use the Stanford Channel Islands chart.

a At 0900 a vessel is at the North cardinal buoy off St Malo entrance (position 48°42.3'N, 2°9.5'E).

i What true course should she set for Le Videcoq Buoy which lies about 4 M West of Pointe du Roc and about 20 m ENE of her position if the tide is setting 330°T at 2 kts? Her planned speed is 5 kts.

ii What is her ground speed?

iii What is her ETA (estimated time of arrival)?

b If in question **a** above, she reduces her planned speed to 4 kts

i What course should she now set?

ii What now is her ground speed?

iii What will be her new ETA?

Answers to Chapter 8

Exercise 1

a 354°T 359°C

b 325°T 330°C

Exercise 2

a To offset her course, offshore, to allow for the tide setting her into the bay.

b i 49°36.7'N 2°3.2'W   **ii** 181 T   **iii** 8.3 kts
c 49°27'N 2°8.1'W
d 273°T 3.4 M
e 130°T 4.2 kts

Exercise 3
a 48°55.9'N 2°32.4'W (NB 2 hr vectors)
b Distance covered = 14.2 M. Therefore ground speed = 7.1 kts.

Exercise 4
a i 092°T   **ii** 4.3 kts   **iii** 1334
b i 098°T   **ii** 3.2 kts   **iii** 1509

Navigation and sound signals in restricted visibility

Fog

Sea fog is probably the most dangerous of all weather conditions that a yachtsman will encounter. It arises when warm moist air flows over cold water. It comes up quite suddenly and some areas, the southern North Sea for instance, are more prone to it than others. Another peculiarity of sea fog as opposed to land fog is that it is quite often accompanied by a breeze.

Two main **dangers** exist in fog:

- You may run aground.

- You may be in collision with another vessel.

They are both equally disastrous. In addition prompt rescue is made much more difficult because of the reduced visibility. Fog therefore is not to be treated lightly.

Navigation in conditions of restricted visibility must be performed with great care. It is essential to keep a constant and careful lookout. You must reduce speed: a useful guideline here is that you should keep your speed down so that you can **stop** *within one half of your visible range*. (ie half the distance that you can see). If visibility is so reduced that in order to maintain a safe speed, you cannot maintain steerage way, then you are strongly advised to *anchor*, if your position permits this. You should not of course, anchor in shipping lanes.

You should ensure that the radar reflector is correctly hoisted (ie in the 'rain catching' position, *not* suspended from one of its corners). Vessels equipped with a radar system are **obliged to maintain a radar watch** in restricted visibility.

It is important to navigate as accurately as possible and to establish your position with some certainty. To do this, use whatever means are available to the vessel: compass, log, echo-sounder, lead-line, Decca, Satnav, RDF etc. In such conditions the folly of using out-dated charts is made obvious. It is also important, if you continue to make way, that the engine is ready for instant use. This raises a question, in that, if the engine is left running it may not enable other sounds to be heard; another vessel, waves breaking on rocks or on-shore for instance. It is necessary therefore to exercise judgement in order to maintain the most effective listening watch possible and to have the vessel ready for instant manoeuvre.

Sound signals appropriate to the type of vessel should be sounded (one long blast followed by two short blasts, morse D for a vessel under sail). On hearing a sound signal for'ard of your position, reduce your speed to an absolute minimum or **stop**, sound your own sound signal and, if you are still making way, proceed with extreme caution until the risk of collision is past. Beware, however, of relying upon the direction of the source of a sound in fog. Sound waves are dispersed, distorted and reflected by moisture in the air and it is very difficult to pinpoint a sound source with any certainty.

When 'coasting' it is prudent to take frequent soundings and RDF bearings. On closing land, approach at right angles to the coast, and take full and proper account of tidal streams. It is sensible in a small yacht to keep to shallow water, you are thus less likely to be threatened by large vessels.

In *dense fog* if you are at all unsure of your position you should proceed with extreme caution or **anchor**, but only anchor *away from shipping lanes*. If you choose to anchor, the appropriate signal for a vessel at anchor should be sounded; for a vessel less than 100 metres in length this is a **bell**, sounded for 5 seconds at one minute intervals.

Procedure when Entering Fog

● Slow down to a safe speed.

● Post extra lookouts.

● Establish your position.

● Sound the fog signal.

● Check that the radar reflector is correctly hoisted.

● Have the engine ready for instant use.

● Maintain a radar watch, if radar is fitted.

Sound signals for vessels under way

There are five prescribed sound or fog signals for vessels underway in restricted visibility. These are:

Vessel	*Sound Signal*
Power vessel, under way, making way.	One long, every 2 mins. (Morse T)
Power vessel, under way but **not** making way.	Two long, every 2 mins. (Morse M)
Vessel: Not under command. Restricted in ability to manoeuvre. Constrained by draught. Towing or pushing. Fishing. Sailing.	One long and two short, every 2 mins. (Morse D)
Last vessel of a tow (composite tows are regarded as a power driven vessel.)	One long and three short, every 2 mins. (Morse B)
Pilot vessel on duty.	Four short. (Morse H)

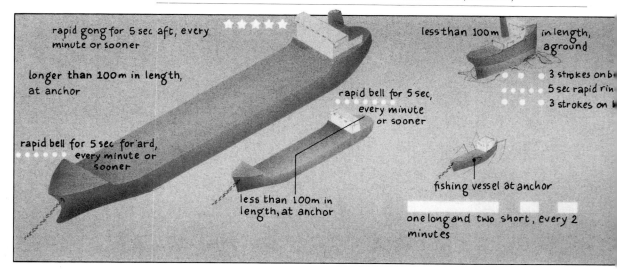

rapid gong for 5 sec aft, every minute or sooner

longer than 100m in length, at anchor

rapid bell for 5 sec for'ard, every minute or sooner

rapid bell for 5 sec, every minute or sooner

less than 100m in length, at anchor

less than 100m in length, aground

3 strokes on b
5 sec rapid rin
3 strokes on b

fishing vessel at anchor

one long and two short, every 2 minutes

Sound signals for vessels at anchor or aground

There are a second group of sound or fog signals for vessels at anchor or aground. These are:

Vessel	Signal
Less than 100m in length, at anchor	Rapid bell for 5 seconds, every minute, or sooner.
Greater than 100m in length, at anchor.	Rapid bell for'ard for 5 secs. Rapid gong aft for 5 seconds. Every minute, or sooner.
Less than 100m in length, aground.	3 strokes on bell, 5 secs rapid ringing on bell, 3 strokes on bell. Every minute, or sooner.
Greater than 100m in length, aground.	3 strokes on bell, 5 seconds on bell, 3 strokes on bell, 5 secs on gong aft, (May also sound the appropriate whistle signal). Every minute, or sooner.
At anchor giving warning of position.	Signal for a vessel at anchor followed by one short, one long and one short blast on the whistle. (Morse R)
Pilot vessel at anchor.	Signal for a vessel at anchor and four short blasts on the whistle. (Morse H)
Fishing vessel at anchor.	Same sound signal as under way. One long and two short blasts. Every 2 mins or sooner.
Restricted in ability to manoeuvre, at work.	Same sound signal as under way. One long and two short blasts. Every 2 mins or sooner.

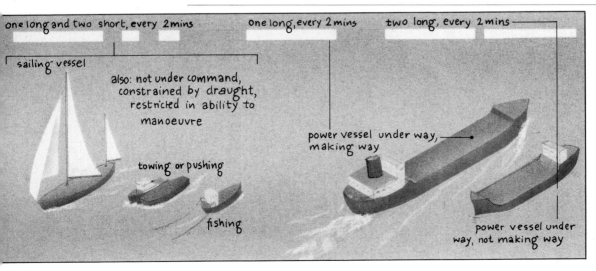

one long and two short, every 2 mins — one long, every 2 mins — two long, every 2 mins

sailing vessel

also: not under command, constrained by draught, restricted in ability to manoeuvre

towing or pushing

fishing

power vessel under way, making way

power vessel under way, not making way

83

Manoeuvring and warning sound signals

There are also a number of sound signals used to indicate to other craft a vessel's intentions. These are:

Sound Signal	Meaning
One short blast. (Morse E)	I am altering course to starboard.
Two short blasts. (Morse I)	I am altering course to port.
Three short blasts. (Morse S)	I am operating astern propulsion.
Five short blasts. (Morse 5)	What are your intentions?
Two long and one short blast. (Morse G)	I intend to overtake on your starboard side.
Two long and two short blasts. (Morse Z)	I intend to overtake on your port side.
One long, one short, one long, one short. (Morse C)	Agreement by the vessel which is to be overtaken.
One long blast.	Vessel nearing a blind bend in a channel. Repeated by a vessel on the other side of the bend.

a What are the two main dangers that exist in fog?

b What is a safe speed in fog?

c How should a radar reflector be positioned for maximum effectiveness?

d What briefly are the actions that you should initiate when entering fog?

e If you are unsure of your position in dense fog, how should you proceed?

f What sound signal would the last vessel in a tow, sound?

g What type of vessel would sound one long and two short blasts?

h What sound is used in restricted visibility by a vessel less than 100 metres in length when aground?

i You are approaching a deep water harbour, in a buoyed channel, when a large vessel astern sounds five short blasts on his whistle. What action should you take?

j If in **i** above, the large vessel now sounds two long blasts and two short blasts on his whistle.

1 What are his intentions?

2 What reply should you make?

a **i** You may run aground.   **ii** You may collide with another vessel.

b That which enables you to stop within half the visible distance.

c In the rain catching position.

d Slow down to a safe speed, post extra lookouts, establish your position, sound the fog signal, check that the radar reflector is correctly hoisted, have the engine ready for instant use, maintain a radar watch (if radar is fitted.)

e With extreme caution.

f One long and three short blasts. Morse B.

g Vessels: not under command, restricted in ability to manoeuvre, constrained by draught, towing or pushing, fishing, sailing.

h She should sound a bell for 5 seconds at one minute intervals.

i Get out of the way. Turn to starboard and sound one short blast.

j **1** She intends to overtake you on your port side.

   2 Sound one long, one short, one long and one short blast. Remember that although she is the overtaking vessel, she is likely to be restricted by her draft to the buoyed channel.

Chapter

Anchoring

The four most common types of anchor used on small craft are the Fisherman, the Danforth or Meon, the CQR or Plough and the Bruce. These are illustrated below together with summaries of their relative merits and disadvantages.

Fisherman   This has poor holding 'power to weight ratio'. It is easily fouled by the warp or cable getting twisted around the upper fluke. Care should also be taken to ensure that the vessel does not take the bottom over such an anchor. It is however, relatively easy to stow, because the stock folds. It is also the only type of anchor which will hold at all well on a rocky seabed, but it must be heavy to be effective.

Danforth or Meon   This has a relatively good holding power to weight ratio and stows away fairly easily. It is not good in thick weed as the flukes do not penetrate well. The crown pivot can also become clogged and by preventing proper deployment of the anchor, reduces its holding power to no more than its weight and that of the cable.

CQR or Plough   This has a reasonably good holding power to weight ratio, but its shape makes it awkward to handle and difficult to stow on deck. These anchors have also been known to fail at the pivot between the plough and stock. An occasional check at that point is to be recommended. The initials *CQR* are an abbreviation for *Anchor, Coastal, Quick Release*.

Bruce   This type of anchor was developed for use on oil-rigs. It digs in well and is firm when the pull is always in the same direction. It tends to pull out rather easily however, when subjected to sideways pull. Being a one-piece anchor it is fairly easy to handle but, it does not stow very easily.

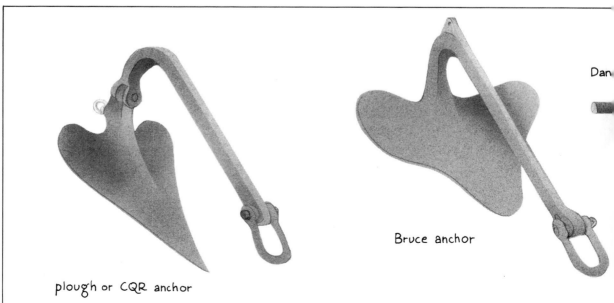

plough or CQR anchor

Bruce anchor

Dan

Cables and Warps   The length or scope of cable or warp to use when anchoring will depend upon:

- The depth of water.
- The intended length of stay.
- The nature of the bottom.
- The strength of the tide.
- The strength and direction of the wind, the expected weather and the available shelter.

In moderate weather, the scope of *cable* veered (paid out), should not be less than *three* times the depth of high water. When using *warp*, which is lighter, it would be necessary to veer *five* times the high water depth. In rough weather, strong tides or where the holding ground is poor, greater lengths should be paid out.

Nylon warps are used for anchoring because of the inherent elasticity of nylon rope and *they stretch*. They should however, be connected to the anchor by at least four metres of cable, the weight of which will cause the anchor to lay flat on the bottom and thus 'bite' when subjected to a horizontal pull.

Holding ground   Hard mud provides the best holding qualities, this is followed by soft mud, sand, shingle and then gravel in decreasing holding power. Rock provides unreliable holding ground and the presence of weed over any ground will worsen the holding quality.

Choice of Anchorage

When choosing an anchorage select an area clear of shipping lanes and where there are no underwater obstructions, wreckage, or mooring lines etc. Do not anchor off a lee-shore. Lay out sufficient cable to allow for the rise of tide. Make allowance for the swing to the anchor with the turn of the tide; lay out an extra anchor if necessary. Make allowance for any expected change in the weather; wind direction and strength for instance.

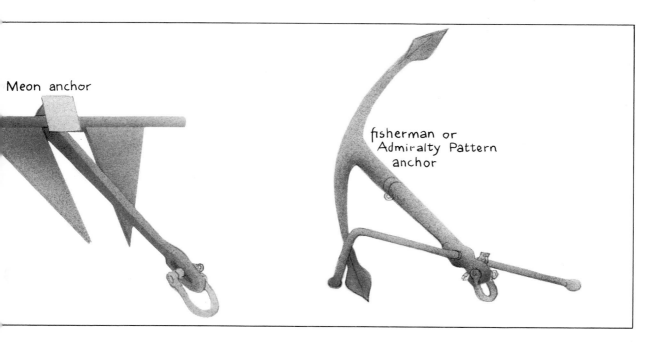

Meon anchor

fisherman or
Admiralty Pattern
anchor

To lay out an Anchor

Flake out the required length of cable on deck. This will depend upon the range and depth of tide and the quality of the seabed. Make sure that the 'bitter end' (that end remote from the anchor) is made fast. Approach the mooring from downstream. Let go the anchor at the chosen spot but 'check' the cable when the anchor touches the bottom. When checking or stopping a cable, do it with a stopper or your boot. (**Never with your hands**) Do not let all the cable go at this point. It will simply foul the flukes and your anchor will break-out. Motor astern or drift back on the tide, paying out the cable as you go. Make the cable fast to the bitt or cleat.

Riding to a Single Anchor

This requires considerable room when swinging with the tide and is suitable only for short periods; Vessels so anchored should not be left unattended.

Buoying the Anchor

An anchor buoy is used to provide a means of freeing the anchor if it should foul an obstruction on the sea bed. The arrangement as shown is effective, but has certain disadvantages, particularly in crowded anchorages. The buoy line may become entangled in the propeller of a passing craft, or even in the yacht's own propeller, when weighing anchor. It is not unknown for a late arrival to make fast to an anchor buoy for an overnight mooring!

There is some advantage therefore in securing the anchor buoy close alongside your vessel and to use a longer tripping line, stopped to the cable with light lashings. This reduces the danger of entanglement but uses a much longer tripping line and the complication of stopping it to the anchor cable makes anchoring more difficult.

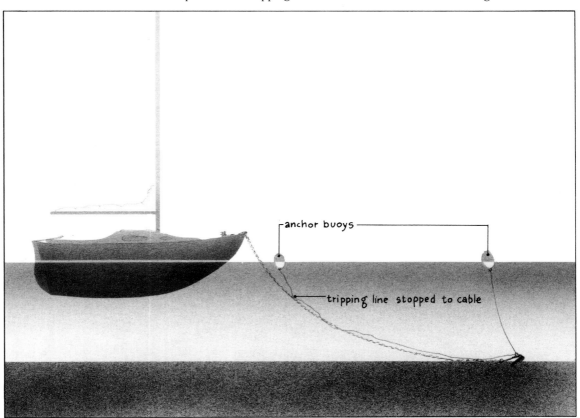

Mooring with Two Anchors

The heaviest anchor should take the greatest strain and in tidal waters the anchors should lie with the direction of the flood and the ebb, one each side of the berth.

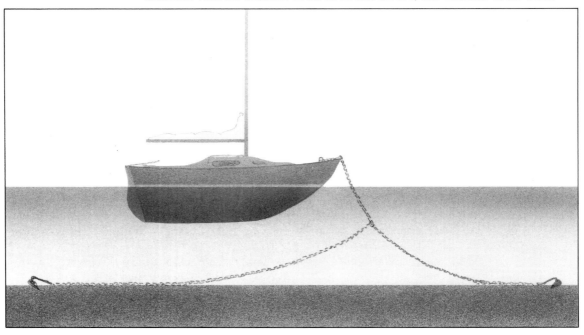

To Lay out Two Anchors   Stem the tide (ie approach the mooring from downstream). Motor just past your selected berth. Drop the first anchor and then fall back on the tide, veering *double* the amount of cable to which you intend to ride. Drop the second anchor. Haul in on the first cable until in your selected position. Shackle the cable of the second anchor to that of the first. Veer out until the second cable is well below the water line. You should now be lying about midway between the anchors, one upstream and the other downstream.

To Free a Fouled Anchor

If no tripping line is rigged there are various methods used to free a fouled anchor. The cable can be hauled up tight (short stay) and a chain ring or necklace passed around the cable. The 'ring' is then lowered on a separate warp to the anchors' crown. Tension on the main cable is eased and the warp attached to the 'ring' hauled up, hopefully freeing the anchor. It may be necessary to haul on the second line (drag line) from the dinghy, but this should be done with care, it is not difficult to capsize a dinghy in these circumstances.

To Raise or Weigh an Anchor

This needs to be done with care. In any sort of a blow or tide the tension on an anchor chain can be considerable and fingers can be lost! If a windlass is used there is less risk of this happening but, in any event, the operation calls for *good communication* between the helmsman and the foredeck anchor party. Misunderstandings occur when the anchor party yell into the wind and over the bow, that the d... .d thing is stuck, particularly when the skipper is all set to go and can't hear a thing over the noise of the engine anyway!

It is much easier to have somebody at the mast, if possible, to relay the polite parts of the messages passed to and fro.

There are also 'prescribed' nautical terms used to describe the various aspects of weighing anchor. Using these could avoid confusion and might lull spectators into thinking that you really know what you are doing!

Short stay	The anchor is said to be at short stay when the cable is more or less parallel with the forestay.
Up and down	Indicates that the cable is vertical.
Anchor aweigh	Indicates that the anchor has just broken out of the sea bed.
Hove in sight	The anchor is just below the surface.
Anchor secure	Means just that

When weighing anchor, have a bucket and a scrubber handy to clean off the cable as it comes aboard. If you stow it in a dirty condition your vessel ere long, will not smell as sweet as she could!

Exercise 1

a Compare the advantages of a CQR against a Fisherman anchor for a 30ft yacht.

b What length of cable would you veer in calm weather on a muddy anchorage, if chart datum was 2.5m and the next high water was forecast to be 5.7m?

c Under what conditions would you consider it necessary to lay out two anchors?

d When is an anchor said to be at 'short stay'?

e What equipment should an anchor party have to hand when weighing the anchor?

Answers to Chapter 10

a The CQR has good power to weight ratio and is a good general purpose anchor. It is not very effective in weed or in rock, unlike the Fisherman anchor which is the most effective of all anchors in rock. Rock, however, is an unreliable holding ground regardless of which anchor is used. The CQR does not handle or stow easily whereas the Fisherman anchor folds flat and is quite reasonable to handle and stow.

b $3 \times 8.2 = 24.6$m.

c In a crowded anchorage where there is insufficient room to swing. In heavy weather.

d When the anchor cable is aligned with or parallel to, the fore-stay.

e Sea boots, a bucket and scrubber, protection for the hands, foul weather gear if conditions require it.

Behaviour, ensigns and flags

Noise in Anchorages

When a vessel is moored or at anchor, all on board should behave in a polite and courteous manner to other users of the anchorage. This particularly applies to noise. Loud music, shouting and raucous behaviour are what most people are trying to get away from. One should try, particularly when leaving or arriving during the small hours, to do so quietly and efficiently. If you know what you are doing and your crew know what you intend, there is little need for extra, shouted and sometimes frenzied, commands.

When anchoring, leave enough room for your vessel to swing without hitting another. On returning to your vessel, try to prevent your dinghy from bumping into other craft. When snugging down for the night, 'frap' your halyards to keep them clear of the mast. The sort of cacophony that results if you don't, is all very well for a dinghy park, but not good enough for the off-shore sailor.

Trot Mooring

When rafting up alongside another craft, ask permission, put out an adequate number of fenders. Carry out the entire manoeuvre at as **low** a speed as is possible. This can only be done when you approach the mooring from *downstream* ie against the tide. Your crew should be able to step ashore, or onto another craft to make fast, easily, safely and *with dignity*.

When crossing another vessel, do so across the forepeak, never across her cockpit. Take your own bow and stern lines ashore; do not rely upon another vessel's warps.

The same recommendations apply when mooring to buoys or piles. The golden rule is:

Do it slowly, do it quietly!!

Racing Yacht Priorities

The act of flying a racing flag does **not** enable you to assume that the 'Rules for the Prevention of Collision at Sea' do not apply! However, other vessels invariably and without obligation, give way to or keep clear of, yachts that are racing. This is an act of courtesy. It is also good common sense. By the same token, the use of a racing flag is *not* to be abused or flown when it might give rise to confusion. The flag is *rectangular* in shape and is flown at the masthead *in place* of the burgee.

Ensigns, burgees and signal flags

The Ensign The *Red Ensign* is normally flown from a jack-staff on the taff-rail by British yachts and merchant vessels.

The *Blue Ensign* is flown by British registered vessels holding a special warrant, eg customs vessels, service clubs and the like.

The *White Ensign* is flown by the Royal Yacht Squadron and by the Royal Navy. The order in which these are mentioned is quite deliberate and without insult. By a quirk of history the RYS happened to have been flying the White Ensign, as were a

number of other clubs, but they alone declined to change their ensign when the Board of Admiralty decided to adopt the White Ensign for the Royal Navy.

The Union Flag   The Union Flag or Union Jack is only flown by the Royal Yacht and ships of the Royal Navy. It should *never* be flown by merchant ships or yachts.

Courtesy Ensigns   It is customary, though not obligatory, when entering a foreign port to fly that country's ensign from the *port* yardarm. It is not polite to fly any other flag on the same hoist above the courtesy ensign.

Club Burgees   A burgee is a *triangular* flag and is normally flown from the masthead. It can alternatively be flown from the *starboard* yardarm. Most clubs have their own particular burgees.

House Flags   These are private flags, flown originally by shipping companies to indicate company ownership. They are normally large, colourful and rectangular in shape. They should be flown from the *starboard* yardarm. Many individual yacht owners now have and may use, their own house flags.

Signal Flags   These are a special group of coloured flags denoting letters of the alphabet and numerals. They each have special meanings when flown individually or in groups. It is highly desirable to know at least some of the more important meanings. The flags are flown from the *port* yardarm.

C Flag   A rectangular flag having five horizontal bands. The upper and lower bands are coloured blue, the centre band is red and the remainder white. It is the 'affirmative' or 'yes' flag.

N Flag   A rectangular chequered flag having sixteen squares on it. Eight of these squares are blue and the remainder are white. It is the 'negative' or 'no' flag.

Q Flag   Yellow rectangle. This must be flown when entering a foreign port after a voyage from a different country or, on return to the UK when from a foreign port. It indicates that 'the vessel is healthy and requests free pratique.' (Pratique means — licence to hold intercourse with the port after quarantine.) No comment! It indicates to HM Customs, that the vessel has been to foreign parts and requires customs clearance.

W Flag   Rectangular, red, white and blue concentric rectangles, red centre. It indicates 'I require medical assistance.'

U Flag   Rectangular, quartered, red and white. It indicates: 'You are running into danger.'

a What shape is a racing flag?
b Does a racing flag give a vessel priority of passage?
c i   When is a courtesy ensign flown?
   ii From which halyard is it flown?
   iii What other flag may be flown on the same hoist above it?
d i   Under what circumstances would you fly a Yellow rectangular flag?
   ii Which of the international signal flags is yellow and rectangular?
   iii From which yardarm should this flag be flown?
e Which flag would you fly if you required a doctor?

a Rectangular.
b No.
c i   On entering a foreign port.
   ii The port yardarm.
   iii None.

d i On entering a foreign port from another foreign country or, on return to the UK from a foreign port.

ii The Q flag.

iii The port yardarm.

e The W flag.

Safety at sea

The Law at Present

All craft must comply with the requirements of the International Rules for the Prevention of Collision at Sea. Pleasure yachts of 13.7 metres (45 ft) loa and upwards, must also conform to the safety requirements laid down in the merchant Shipping rules 1965. For craft less than 13.7m recommendations exist and these should be followed as far as possible. The RYA booklet G9/81 *Safety Equipment for Cruising Yachts* lists the recommendations for small craft.

Personal Safety

One lifejacket to BS3595 should be carried for each person on board and worn at all times when there is a risk of falling or being pitched into the water. One safety harness to BS4225 should also be carried for each person board and worn at all times when there is a risk of falling overboard, when on deck in bad weather, or at night. If harnesses are worn, speed should be reduced to less than eight knots. A person falling overboard and towed by his harness at a faster speed than this, will almost certainly drown.

In addition, an inflatable liferaft capable of carrying everyone on board should be carried on deck, together with two lifebuoys, one fitted with a self-igniting light and the other with a smoke float and 30 metres of buoyant line.

The above items of equipment are of course additional to distress flares and normal items of equipment such as anchors, compass, tow rope, first aid kit, radio, radar reflector, torch, lifelines etc.

When sailing in estuaries and inland waters a buoyancy aid may be substituted for the lifejacket. The basic difference between the two is, that the buoyancy aid is intended to assist a swimmer to remain afloat, whereas a BS lifejacket will support an unconscious person in the water keeping the mouth and nose above water.

Lifejackets should be worn:

- By non-swimmers at all times when on deck.

- In dinghies, particularly in heavy weather.

- When there is a higher than normal risk of having to abandon ship (ie in very severe weather or in fog).

- When working outside the guardrails (ie working on a mooring buoy).

Man Overboard Drill

Every person aboard a small craft must be thoroughly conversant with the *Man Overboard drill*.

- As soon as a person observes that somebody has gone overboard, that person must shout **Man overboard** and must then point to and *not* take his eyes off the person in the water. This is *most important*.

- Then get a lifebuoy or danbuoy over the side as quickly and as close to the victim as possible.

- On hearing the shout, it is a case of 'all Hands on deck'.
- You must now get the vessel back quickly and to windward of the victim and whilst doing it, position the person 'pointing' so that he has maximum visibility; by the mast is a good place.
- There are numerous ways of getting the vessel back quickly, each has its advocates, but all must take account of the prevailing conditions. The main thing is, that it is done quickly and safely, for in very cold weather survival time in the water is measured in minutes and not too many at that.
- It now remains to retrieve the victim. Get a line to him quickly and then use whatever means you have devised for getting him back on board. Remember that now he is wet, he will be very heavy, almost twice his normal weight.
- Again there are many advocates of the various ways of getting the man back on board. The main thing is to do it quickly and without injuring him.

In bringing a man back on board, regardless of which method you use, you will invariably find it much easier if the guard rails are first lowered. On a well run vessel the guardrails will be tensioned by lanyards to the sternrail or pushpit. Cut these lanyards quickly and lower the rails. The lanyards are provided for just this purpose; they are also said to improve RDF reception by breaking a continuous electrical loop, but this is a bonus.

Man overboard drill is not a joke. Survival time in the water is short. In darkness and in bad weather it is even more difficult to recover a man overboard. With only two persons on board, the loss of one overboard could be disastrous. Take great care therefore when moving about out of the cockpit and particularly on the foredeck.

Clothing and Working Attitudes

It is important to wear warm clothing and non-slip shoes or sea boots in heavy weather. Even in summer it can be very cold at sea and morale is greatly increased if the crew are warm and dry.

The sea is a dangerous place but, many accidents can be avoided if care and forethought are applied when working. Adopt a working attitude with safety ever uppermost in your mind. Remember, *One hand for yourself and one hand for the ship* is as sound a rule for a small craft sailor today, as it ever was.

When working on the foredeck, sit rather than stand. When going for'ard or moving about out of the cockpit, *hold on*, keep your head down and try to keep to the windward side of the vessel. Mind the boom and the jib on gybes. Do not stand on sails; they are very slippery, particularly when wet. Do not leave handles in the reefing gear or winches; in heavy weather such items can get thrown about and can be very dangerous.

Keep the boat tidy, the falls of halyards should be neatly coiled and stowed, sheets should be neatly coiled in the cockpit; you cannot always predict events which may require sheets and halyards to be let out in a hurry. Coil and stow all warps on leaving harbour, not forgetting to take inboard and stow all fenders.

Exercise 1

a Which craft must comply with the International Regulations for the Prevention of Collisions at Sea?

b How many lifejackets and harnesses are required to be carried on a 30ft yacht?

c What is the recommended size for a liferaft for a 30ft yacht and where should it be carried when under way?

d When should lifejackets be worn?

e Identify three bad practices which, on a foredeck, could lead to a man without a harness, going overboard.

Dinghies

Most boating accidents occur in dinghies. Because of this you should be particularly careful when using one. Make sure that your dinghy has adequate buoyancy. It should never be overloaded and you should never unnecessarily stand up in it; particularly an inflatable. It should be loaded evenly and the weight kept as low as is possible. If you capsize, stay with the boat. It is important to secure the painter inside the dinghy after casting off; otherwise it might foul the propeller of the outboard. This could stall the outboard if you are lucky, or it might, by winding the painter around the prop, change your dinghy into a banana shaped float! Fingers can also be easily injured if trapped between the dinghy and a hard spot; so, keep all fingers inboard, especially the 'little ones'.

Children, Boating and Bathing

Children love messing about in boats and they also seem to move so quickly! They appear to have a built-in lack of fear or danger and in consequence, they *must* be properly supervised. Make sure that they are taught to swim, but regardless of whether they can or not, ensure that they wear a lifejacket or a buoyancy aid. Never allow children to draw water from over the side using a bucket. If they are permitted to play in the dinghy, make sure that it is attached to the boat with a decent painter. Attach the oars, paddles and rowlocks to that they cannot be lost over the side. Only when children have acquired skill and competence, should they be allowed 'off the painter'. If they are permitted to motor the dinghy freely around crowded moorings, impress upon them that noise causes nuisance, but much more importantly, be aware of the danger that could arise if a vessel has to take rapid action to avoid your child in a dinghy!

Bathe in sheltered waters, never in a strong tidal stream. You should avoid swimming alone. If you are swimming from a yacht, have a ladder over the side. Make sure that everyone can swim, if at all possible. Learn artificial respiration, particularly mouth to mouth. Children of course, should be constantly supervised. Secure air beds and floating aids with a line to the boat.

Boat Safety

Before leaving port it is sensible to prepare a navigation plan and essential to check the tides, the weather and the boat. It is also good practice to tell somebody where you are going. There is a coastguard service for this, but do use it sensibly. The coastguard service is very heavily committed. (HM Coastguard Yacht and Boat Safety scheme.)

Probably the worst accident that can befall a small craft at sea is an explosion followed by fire; and the most likely cause of this is fuel or gas leaking from the engine or cooker. In a boat, petrol or bottled gas, spilled or leaked will, because they are heavier than air, flow into the bilges. This can create a highly explosive atmosphere. In a boat with a petrol engine, a drip tray should be fitted under the carburettor. Gas bottles should be carried in a locker which vents or drains overboard.

If you suspect that there are inflammable fumes in the bilges, turn off the cooker and the gas at the bottle, *do not* light any matches or turn any electrical apparatus either *on or off*, either could give rise to a spark. Then pump out the bilges by hand or bale out with a bucket. Then ventilate the vessel thoroughly.

When under way turn the gas off at the bottle, unless the cooker is attended. It is bad practice to leave a lighted cooker unattended; gas flames frequently blow out. When taking over a boat, check the condition of gas feed flexible hoses for evidence of perishing or damage. Check the condition of all gas pipes at least annually.

Fire Extinguishers

Craft up to 9 metres in length, with cooking facilities and an engine on board should carry two 3lb capacity dry powder extinguishers. For craft with larger engines, the size should be increased to 5lb. Maintenance of fire extinguishers should follow the maker's instructions. With simple dry powder extinguishers, it is important to prevent the powder from compacting into a solid lump, by occasionally shaking the extinguisher vigorously.

Two buckets, with lanyards, should also be carried. Water can be used for extinguishing fires in dry solids, such as bedding, but not on liquids such as fat or petrol; water tends to spread the fire. Water should not be used on electrical fires. A fire blanket can also be used for smothering fires in liquids, but it must be left in place until the temperature has reduced sufficiently or the fire may re-ignite.

Seacocks and Bilge Pumps

All hull openings below the waterline should be fitted with seacocks to prevent water siphoning back through the pipe. Seacocks also enable the opening to be closed off in the event of a broken pipe.

Boats should be fitted with two good bilge pumps and the intakes should be fitted with strum boxes. A mixture of electrical and mechanical pumps is quite acceptable, but one pump should be operable from the cockpit and the other from inside the cabin. It should be possible to operate both pumps with all hatches closed.

Exercise 2

a Identify three practices which could be dangerous when using dinghies.
b The safety of children on board can be considerably enhanced by implementing two rules. What are they?
c How many bilge pumps are required for a 30ft yacht?
d What is the main function of a seacock?
e What firefighting equipment should a 30ft yacht carry?
f How would you extinguish a fat fire in the galley in a frying pan on the cooker?

Distress Signals

Distress signals should only be used when the **vessel** and crew is in grave and immediate danger.

The principal method of signalling distress on a modern vessel is by **VHF** using the *Mayday* procedure. Although the use of VHF is restricted to licenced operators, it can be safely assumed, particularly on a small vessel, that in the *event of distress* and the licenced operator being indisposed, anybody can make the distress call.

It is however most important when sending a distress call, to use the *correct procedure*. This procedure is internationally used, and has been devised to enable all the relevant information to be transmitted rapidly and in an 'agreed format'.

Mayday Procedure

1 Switch on the VHF set, switch to high power (25 watts) and select **Channel 16**.

2 *Listen* to ensure that the channel is free.

3 *Think* precisely of what you are about to say.

4 Hold the microphone firmly, press the transmit button. (*NB* It is vital that the *press to transmit* button is held down *only* when you intend to transmit. To do so at any other time will block the channel and you will not be able to receive an answer to your call and, more importantly, your chances of rescue are considerably diminished.) Send the following message.

5 Mayday, mayday, mayday

This is (yacht) (Boatname) (Boatname) (Boatname)

Mayday (Boatname)

My position is: Lat/long or, x miles, bearing *FROM* (Shore land mark)

My vessel is (state the problem: struck object, on fire etc)

I require (state your needs: immediate assistance etc)

There are: (No. of people) on board. Other information (we are taking to the liferaft etc).

Mayday (Boatname)

Over

6 *Release* the transmit button.

7 Listen for a reply. If none is heard within about a minute, check the equipment (you may still be holding down the transmit button!) and try again. Remember, your vessel is in *Grave and Imminent Danger*, you are not going to have much time to check thoroughly.

If you are in sight of land or another vessel at the time, your distress can be signalled by *distress flares* or by *visual signals*. Losing a man overboard, even the skipper, is *not* a *distress* situation as such. To summon assistance in such a situation a **Pan Pan** call would be broadcast; should the circumstances demand it. Procedures for VHF operation will not be dealt with in depth here. The correct procedures are however laid down and a licence of competence to operate must be held. This can be obtained by tuition and examination at an approved place of instruction.

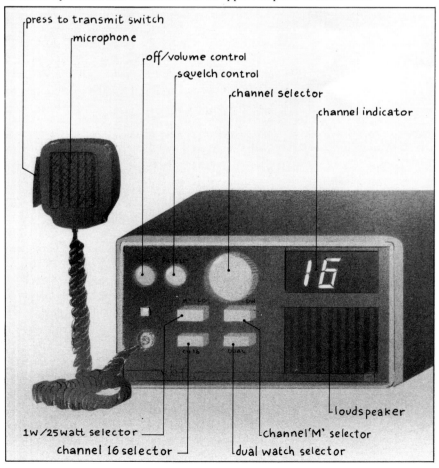

press to transmit switch

microphone

off/volume control

squelch control

channel selector

channel indicator

loudspeaker

1W/25 watt selector

channel 16 selector

channel 'M' selector

dual watch selector

Distress Flares

Usage To use distress flares in coastal waters in an emergency, let off two flares in the same direction, within about two minutes of each other, wait a while and then let two more off. Keep back at least one red handflare (in darkness, gale or poor visibility) or orange smoke (for daylight in light winds) to signal your position to approaching rescuers. Be sure to hold flares well away from the body and point them downwind.

Finally make sure that you know how to use all of the equipment *before* an emergency arises. There will not be time to read the instructions at the time.

Types of Flare The various types of distress flare (pyrotechnic) to be found on small craft are as follows:

A Red Rocket Parachute Flare. Used to give the longest possible range alarm signal.

Hand Held Red Flare. Used to pinpoint the position of a vessel in distress when help is on the way, or as an alarm signal over a relatively short distance.

Orange Smoke (buoyant or hand-held). An alternative to the hand-held red flare; more effective in bright light and light wind. Particularly useful when signalling to aircraft.

Two-Star Red Signal. Now difficult to obtain. Used as a medium range alarm signal. Particularly useful when a parachute rocket, which is projected to great height, might be obscured by low cloud.

Requirements for Small Craft *Small Craft,* within 3 miles off-shore should carry 2 red hand flares and 2 orange smoke signals.

Larger yachts in coastal waters, up to 7 miles from land, should carry 4 two-star red signals in addition to 4 red handflares and 2 orange smoke signals.

Offshore, more than 7 miles out, 4 parachute rockets should replace the two-star signals recommended for coastal use.

White hand flares are carried for use as collision warnings.

Other Methods of Signalling

All the above methods of signalling distress are listed in the Collision Regulations (Annex V.) For small vessels however, if pyrotechnics are not available, the following alternatives can be used to indicate distress:

- A square flag hoisted over a ball.

- An N flag over a C flag on the same hoist.

- An ensign hoisted upside down.

- An ensign made fast in the rigging.

- An article of clothing put up on an oar.

- Waving your outstretched arms slowly up and down.

- Continuous loud noise; a fog horn for instance.

- Burning a barrel of tar on deck (not easy to find or to be recommended on a small yacht).

If not in distress, but needing assistance, a **Pan Pan** call can be transmitted on VHF. Alternatives are to signal V in morse ($\cdot\cdot-$) or hoist the V flag.

For medical assistance a **Pan Pan Medico** signal can be sent on VHF. Alternatives are to signal W ($\cdot--$) or hoist the W flag.

One should also look out for the signal U ($\cdot\cdot-$) 'You are running into danger.'

Answering Signals

Answering signals made by lifeboat stations when distress signals are seen are:

In daylight, an orange smoke signal.

At night, three white star rockets fired at one minute intervals.

Exercise 3

a List the contents of a Mayday signal.

b When should a Mayday signal be used?

c What form of VHF signal is sent when a man lost overboard, cannot be located?

d What range of pyrotechnics should an offshore yacht carry?

e List six methods of signalling distress at sea.

f What VHF signal is sent for medical assistance?

g Your vessel is 3 miles offshore and collides with a submerged object at night. You are taking water faster than it can be pumped out. Your VHF set has been swamped and is now unserviceable. What do you do?

h What signal would be sent from the shore at night, to acknowledge receipt of a distress signal?

Answers to Chapter 12

Exercise 1

a All craft.

b One lifejacket and one harness for each person on board.

c **i** Of a size that it is capable of carrying everybody on board.

ii On deck, when underway.

d **i** By non-swimmers at all times when on deck.

ii In dinghies, particularly in heavy weather.

iii When there is a higher than normal risk of having to abandon ship (ie in very severe weather or in fog).

iv When working outside the guardrails (ie working on a mooring buoy).

e **i** Treading on sails.

ii Going for'ard without holding on.

iii Tripping over loose halyards or sheets.

iv Wearing inadequate footwear and slipping.

v Being swept over by the jib.

vi Not paying attention to what is going on.

Exercise 2

a **i** Overloading.

ii Standing up.

iii Trailing the painter.

iv Making the craft top heavy.

b **i** To ensure that they are properly supervised.

ii To ensure that unless they are ashore or below, they always wear their lifejackets.

c Two.

d To close off an opening in the hull.

e Two 3 lb dry powder extinguishers. Two buckets with lanyards. A fire blanket.

f Exclude air, smother with a fire blanket. Do **not** attempt to throw the burning fat over the side.

Exercise 3

a Switch to Ch 16, high power and then listen. Then transmit:

Mayday, 3 times

Boatname 3 times

Mayday, Boatname.

My position is . . .

My problem is . . .
I require assistance.
There are X people on board.
We are taking to the liferaft or whatever.
Mayday, boatname.
Over.
Release the transmitter button and listen for a reply.

b When a vessel is in grave and imminent danger.

c A Pan Pan signal.

d 4 parachute rocket flares, 4 red hand flares, 2 orange smoke and 2 white hand flares.

e Red rockets, red flares, orange smoke, a square flag hoisted over a ball, an N flag over a C flag on the same hoist, an ensign hoisted upside down, an ensign made fast in the rigging, an article of clothing put up on an oar, waving your outstretched arms slowly up and down, continuous loud noise, on a fog horn for instance, burning a barrel of tar on deck.

f Pan Pan Medico.

g Don life jackets and then fire off two red parachute flares, or two red hand flares at two minute intervals; it may be necessary to repeat this signal but try to keep one flare in reserve. Alternatively signal S O S (dit dit dit, dah dah dah, dit dit dit) by light to the shore. Prepare to take to the liferaft.

h Three white star rockets at one minute intervals.

Meteorology

Weather

Of all the factors which affect or influence the safety and performance of a vessel at sea, the weather is probably the most significant and the least predictable. Your margins of safety can be increased considerably if you are able to correctly interpret weather patterns, cloud formations and the variations of pressure and temperature. To do this with any confidence it is necessary to acquire a basic understanding of weather systems and of how they originate and move.

Air Masses

Weather systems develop from the interaction and movement of cold and warm air masses. The cold masses develop at the Poles and the warm in the Tropics. They develop in consequence of contact with Earth's surface and are cooled or heated accordingly. The transfer of heat is a slow process taking several days, sometimes weeks, to accomplish.

Cold Air Masses The characteristics of a cold air mass are;

● Low temperature.

● Low moisture content.

● A small temperature gradient, with height.

The tracks of *all* cold air masses are towards warmer regions.

Warm Air Masses Warm Air Masses are of two types.
a Tropical *maritime* air masses which have high temperatures, high moisture content and a relatively low temperature gradient with height.
b Tropical *continental* air masses which have very high temperatures, especially at the lower levels and very low moisture content.

   The tracks of all tropical air masses are towards higher latitudes. This results in the cooling of the lower layers.

Formation of Pressure Areas

In the summer, large land masses are much warmer than the sea and in winter much colder. In consequence, in the summer the air which is heated by the land rises, and a low pressure area develops. These low pressure areas, which form over the continental land masses, affect our weather system. They occur in the main over Iceland; due to the heating of the south moving polar air mass and over central Europe; due to a combination of the heating of cold and tropical continental air masses.

   The heated air rises to a higher altitude, where it then cools and descends to other places on the Earth's surface. At such places high pressure areas develop. In the summer the Azores is a place where high pressures frequently develop. The Azores region lies to the west of a midway point between the American and European continental masses.

   In winter, the low temperatures of the European continental mass, cause air to descend and in consequence, high pressure areas form readily over Europe in the winter. This in turn causes an overall change in the distribution of pressure areas and the Azores High invariably moves further south, with a corresponding deterioration in our local weather.

Movement and Rotation of Air Masses

The interactive effect of a low pressure area over Iceland and a high pressure area over the Azores would, in the absence of other forces, cause air to flow directly from the high to the low pressure area. Because of the many other forces, which combine in a variety of ways, the flow is *not* direct. It is affected by the rotation of the Earth for instance; this imparts a higher velocity to an air mass at the Equator than it does at a higher latitude.

This is because the circumference of the earth at the equator is about 24,000 miles whereas at 50°N it is only a little over 16,000 miles. As the Earth rotates once in 24 hours, its speed at the equator is about 24,000 miles in 24 hours, ie 1,000 mph approx. At 50°N however its speed is only 16,000 miles in 24 hours, ie 666 mph approx. This difference in speed will in consequence have a greater effect on air flowing from the equator than it will on air flowing from the pole and will impart an *anti-clockwise* motion to air masses in the Northern hemisphere. It does however have a very much greater effect on a Low pressure area than it does on a high. So much so in fact, that the Low itself imparts a clockwise motion to the high.

Low Pressure Areas

Consider water in a basin which is flowing out through a plug-hole. The movement of water at the centre is much greater than at the outside. A *low pressure* area can be likened to an inverted plug-hole; but instead of water we have air, and it *rises* at the centre. The air at the centre of a low comes from all points but always from higher pressure areas. In the diagram below;

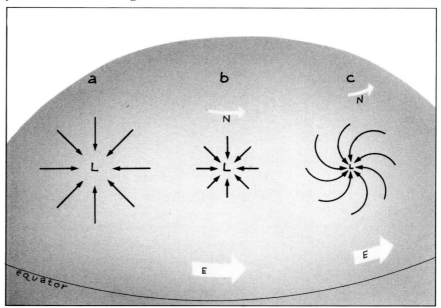

At **a** the air is shown flowing directly towards the *low*, as it would with no other influences.

At **b** the arrows E and N represent respectively, the movement of the Earth at the equator and at a more northerly latitude. It has been shown above that the speed at the equator is greater than at 50°N and in consequence the effect at the equator is greater and the air is moved in an anti-clockwise direction. This movement continues to develop until as shown at –

c all the air around the low is rotating in an anti-clockwise direction.

To summarise, the air around a *low* pressure area moves in an *anti-clockwise* direction and flows in a spiral towards the centre of the low. Low pressure areas are known as *cyclones*. (In the Southern hemisphere, the rotation of produced by the same effect is clockwise. These notes however will concentrate on the effects in our northern weather system.)

High Pressure Areas

The diagram below illustrates how the rotational effect of the low pressure area imparts a clockwise movement to the air mass around the high.

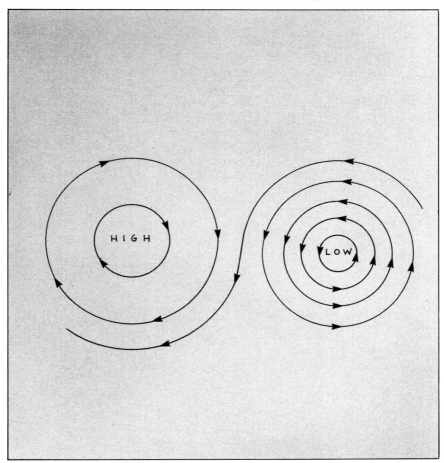

To summarise, the air around a *high* pressure area rotates in a *clockwise* direction and flows in a spiral, outwards from the centre of the high. High pressure areas are known as *anti-cyclones*.

Atlantic Lows

In the Atlantic weather system, areas of low pressure tend to form along the Polar Front. This front is the boundary between the cold polar air stream and the warm tropical air stream. The low pressure areas form and deepen as they move along this boundary in an easterly direction.

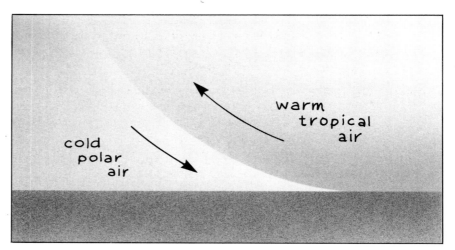

Warm and Cold Fronts

Most of the frontal depressions which affect the British Isles, originate either in the south west Atlantic or off the east coast of America. The precise manner in which these lows form is most complex, but basically the cold dense air from the Polar regions meets the warmer tropical air moving north and moves in underneath it. This in turn pushes the moist warm air upwards.

This gives rise to an unstable condition which is further influenced by local hot-spots and causes small low pressure areas to form. This effect is illustrated in the diagram below at A.

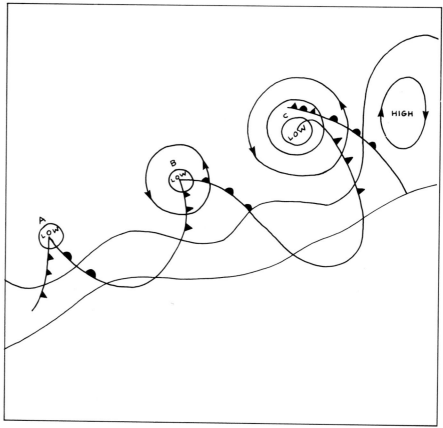

These small low pressure areas combine and the low deepens and as the air mass rotates, a warm edge or front is formed; this is followed by a faster moving cold front, as shown at B. The cold front eventually overtakes the warm front and an occluded front is formed as shown at C.

Exercise 1

a What are the characteristics of a cold air mass?
b Name two types of warm air mass.
c In which direction do warm air masses move?
d What type of pressure system is an anti-cyclone?

Weather and Frontal Systems

An approaching frontal system will cause weather conditions to change. In order to safeguard your vessel and crew, you should be able to recognise and act upon the effects arising from changing cloud formations, atmospheric pressure and temperature. A typical frontal system has the attributes illustrated below:

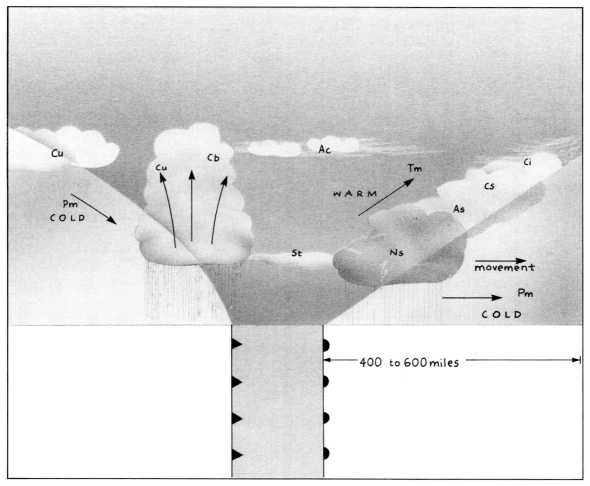

	Cold front	**Warm front**	
Clear, good visibility	Wind veers to W or NW	Wind veers to SW and freshens	Poor visibility
Pressure rises slowly	Pressure rises sharply	Pressure steady, temperature rises	Pressure falls rapidly, temperature steady

111

Weather Forecasts

It is important for the navigator of a small craft to have some idea of what weather he may expect on a certain passage. On this will depend, firstly whether it is prudent to undertake such a voyage, and secondly, what course to take. The course taken may however have to be amended during the voyage, if a later weather forecast predicts an adverse change in conditions.

You should not normally be caught out by bad weather, but if you are, then keep well away from a lee shore, and snug the vessel down. If you are making for a port or anchorage in order to shelter, then do so in plenty of time.

Weather Maps

Synoptic diagrams are a special form of map on which areas of equal pressure are joined by lines known as isobars. The density or compression of isobars over any area is an indication of the wind strength at that place (ie more bars, more wind!) The interval between isobars is a matter of choice and is determined by the scale of the chart and the amount of detail required; 2-millibar intervals are adequate for local area diagrams. Newspaper charts invariably use 8 mbar intervals for the Atlantic chart and 4 mbar for the British Isles.

Warm fronts are identified on synoptic charts by semi-circular marks along the line of the front. Cold fronts are identified by sharp pointed triangular marks.

A typical synoptic diagram is illustrated opposite and such a diagram can be constructed from the information contained in the Shipping Forecast broadcast on Radio 4. It is not intended to cover the construction of synoptic diagrams in this text, this is very adequately covered elsewhere.* It is intended however, to briefly cover how the information in the chart is used to forecast the weather. Assume that in the weather forecast broadcast, the general synopsis stated that 'the Low 998 currently over SW Ireland would move ENE and would be at German Bight the same time tomorrow.'

In the diagram above this point is shown as X and the low is expected to move along the straight line to X in the next 24 hours (ie same time tomorrow). As the low moves along the line, so also will all the weather associated with it. Similarly all the weather along line A-B will also move, with the low. An observer at point P therefore will experience all the weather between point P and point A (the distance A-P is the same as from X to the centre of the low).

The forecast for point P will then be; SSW winds (at the strength now experienced) for about 7 hours; visibility will deteriorate and peristent rain will commence, becoming heavy; the temperature will be steady but the pressure will fall quite rapidly. This weather will last until the warm front passes through. At that time the wind will veer to WSW and freshen; the pressure will remain steady and the temperature will rise. The rain will then ease but the sky will remain overcast. In about 12 hours time the rain will become very heavy and the wind will freshen and veer NW; the pressure will rise sharply and the temperature will fall, as the cold front passes through. Behind the cold front, the pressure will rise slowly, the temperature will steady and visibility will become good. This forecast is of course based upon a very simple weather system and presumes that nothing untoward occurs to disturb it; in practice however, such is not often the case, but the same principles apply when interpreting a weather chart.

Forecasting Instruments

The barometer and, to a lesser extent, the thermometer, are the two most useful instruments for forecasting the weather. By carefully watching and recording the barometer regularly, it should be possible to anticipate the approach of a low pressure

* *Weather For Sailing* (Stanford Maritime) £5.95.

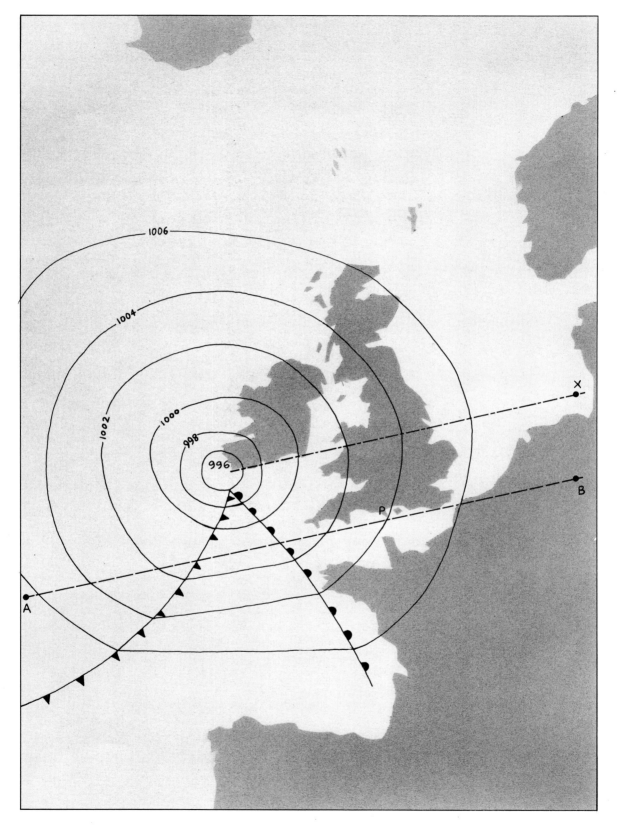

system. Low pressure systems usually bring about a strong increase in the force of the wind.

Exercise 2 **a** Describe the expected weather conditions during the approach and passage of a warm front.

b Describe the expected weather conditions during the approach and passage of a cold front.

c What shift of wind will occur if the centre of a low pressure area passes;

i To the south of your position?

ii Over your position?

iii To the north of your position?

d In the absence of radio and any other communication to the shore, what means would you employ to forecast the weather?

Sources of Weather Information

The following sources of weather information are available to the coastal yachtsman:

- *Weather maps in local newspapers* These give good background information on the local weather situation but suffer from the length of time between drawing the map and its publication.

- *Shipping forecasts broadcast on Radio 4* These are comprehensive forecasts for general maritime use. Because of the size of each area and the very large area covered, no local variations can be included and they must therefore be deduced by the listener. The broadcast will include any gale warnings, a general synopsis, a forecast for the next 24 hours and the latest reports from coastal stations. The area forecasts give detail on wind, weather and visibility. The 'reports from coastal stations' are timed later than the main chart time and detail wind, weather, visibility, barometric pressure and trend.

- *Coastal Inshore waters forecasts broadcast on Radio 4* These are particularly useful for inshore waters.

- *Land weather forecasts on Radio 4* These give background to the general situation but little information on wind strength and direction.

- *Automatic telephone weather service* Very useful as it is available at any time but gives limited information on wind strength and direction.

- *BBC local radio forecasts for yachtsmen* Varies from area to area. Radio Solent is excellent.

- *Marinecall* A very useful telephone service jointly sponsored and operated by the coastguard, British Telecom and DoT. It covers 13 areas around the British Isles.

- *VHF R/T Channel 28* Broadcast times for specific areas are given in the Nautical Almanacs. Information for the Portland, Wight, Dover areas is broadcast at 0833 and 2033.

Gale Warnings

Gale warnings are issued when winds of at least force 8 or gusts exceeding 43 kts are expected. Severe gales imply winds up to force 9 and gusts reaching 52 kts.

Gale warnings are broadcast on Radio 4 (1500 m or 2000 KHz − Long Wave) as soon as possible after receipt and are repeated on the hour immediately following. They are also broadcast on W/T and R/T by British Telecom as soon after receipt as is practical and on R/T at the next of the following times:

0303   0903   1503 and 2103.

They remain in force unless amended or cancelled. Warnings are re-issued if the gale persists 24 hours after the original time of origin. It is to be remembered that within a storm there can be sudden shifts of wind still at gale force. A gale commencing from SW may shift suddenly to NW.

Terms Used in Broadcasts

The terms used in these broadcasts have the following definitions:

Gale Warnings

Imminent	less than 6 hours.
Soon	between 6 and 12 hours.
Later	more than 12 hours from the time of issue.

Visibility (sea area forecasts)

Good	more than 5 nautical miles.
Moderate	2 to 5 nautical miles.
Poor	1100 yards to 2 nautical miles.
Fog	less than 1100 yards
	(land forecasts, less than 200 yards)
Mist or Haze	1100 to 2200 yards.

Pressure Tendency

	Change
Steady	less than 0.1 mb in last 3 hours
Rising/falling slowly	0.1 to 1.5 mb „ „ „ „
Rising/falling	1.6 to 3.5 mb „ „ „ „
Rising/falling quickly	3.6 to 6.0 mb „ „ „ „
Rising/falling very quickly	more than 6.0 mb in last 3 hours.

A fall in pressure of more than 8 mb in 3 hours is almost certain to result in a gale.

Speed of Movement of Pressure Systems

Slowly	up to 15 kts
Steadily	15–25 Kts
Rather quickly	25–35 Kts
Rapidly	35–45 Kts
Very rapidly	over 45 Kts

Winds

Wind speeds are measured on the Beaufort scale from wind force 0 to wind force 12. The table below gives brief details of wind speed in knots, sea and land terms, sea state and wave heights for the various Beaufort numbers (Bt No. in the table)

Bt No.	Wind Kts	Sea terms	Land terms	Sea state	Wave height avge	max
0	< 1	Calm	Calm	Mirror like.	–	–
1	1–3	Light airs	Light winds	Ripples	–	–
2	4–6	Light breeze	,,	Small wavelets	0.15	0.3
3	7–10	Gentle breeze	,,	Large wavelets, crests begin to break, scattered white horses	0.6	1.0
4	11–16	Moderate breeze	Moderate breeze	Small waves, fairly frequent white horses.	1.0	1.5
5	17–21	Fresh breeze	Fresh	Moderate waves, longer. Many white horses.	1.8	2.5
6	22–27	Strong breeze	,,	Large waves, white foam, crests extensive.	3.0	4.0
7	28–33	Near gale	Strong	Sea heaps up, foam from breaking waves begins in streaks downwind.	4.0	6.0
8	34–40	Gale	Gale	Moderately high waves of greater length. Crests breaking into spindrift. Foam blown in streaks downwind.	5.5	7.5
9	41–47	Strong		High waves. Dense streaks of foam. Wave crests begin to topple. Spray affecting visibility.	7.0	9.8
10	48–55	Storm		Very high waves. Long overhanging crests. Foam in great patches in dense white streaks. Sea appears white.	9.0	12.5
11	56–63	Violent		Exceptionally high waves. Sea completely covered with long white foam patches. Heavy sea tumbling. Visibility affected.	11.3	16.0
12	64 +	Hurricane		Air filled with foam and spray. Sea completely white with driving spray. Visibility seriously affected.	13.7	–

Rigs

The following table lists, as a rough guide only, typical rigs for various wind strengths.

Wind Force		Rig
0–3		Full main and genoa
4–5	11 Kts	Main and jib
6–7	22 ,,	Reef main and No 1 or storm jib
8	34 ,,	Drop main and use storm jib
9	41 ,,	Heave to
10	48 ,,	Survival tactics.

In addition to gales there are other hazardous winds and conditions.

Strong Local Winds   These occur up to 10 miles from the coast, particularly on the edges of anti-cyclones and when the wind blows parallel to the coast. A similar increase in wind strength occurs off prominent cliffs and headlands.

Sea Breezes   Another local wind is the *sea breeze*. This occurs on a summer's day when the dry land is heated more quickly than the sea. The warm air over the land rises and air is drawn in from the sea to replace it. The day starts with a gentle onshore breeze which increases markedly during the day, probably dying out in the late afternoon.

Katabatic Winds   On a clear night adjacent to mountains with steep valleys between them which run down to the waters edge, a strong local offshore wind can occur. This is caused by the katabatic effect of cold air falling into the valleys as they cool. Such winds are known as katabatic winds.

Squalls and Thunderstorms   These are usually seen approaching as an arched line of black cloud. They differ from approaching frontal systems by the lack of a freshening wind and sea ahead of them. In such conditions the barometer reading also becomes erratic.

Fog   Land or radiation fog forms over the land on a clear night and usually drifts 2 or 3 miles out to sea. Sea fog is one of the worst hazards likely to be encountered by the yachtsman. It forms when warm moist air is carried by the wind over a relatively cold sea.

Other Factors and Hazards

When deciding whether or not to put to sea, a number of factors other than wind strength and weather must also be taken into account. Some of these are listed below.

Shelter   An offshore wind will give relatively calm sea conditions, which deteriorate the further off-shore you go.

Tidal Stream   In a wind against tide situation, the waves become shorter and steeper, more white horses are formed and conditions are generally more uncomfortable than in a 'no tide' or 'wind with tide' situation.

Depth of Water   In shallow water the waves are generally steeper than in deep water. They also have a pronounced tendency to break heavily.

Sea Bed   An uneven sea-bed, particularly one with pronounced ledges, will give rise to broken water if there is any tidal stream, and sea conditions will be markedly worse when the wind and tide are in opposite directions.

Crew and Boat Strength   The strength and fitness of the crew and an appreciation of their fatigue and tiredness must always be considered when contemplating putting to sea. The strength and condition of the boat must also be similarly considered.

Exercise 3

a List five sources of weather information.
b When would you expect the arrival of a gale, forecast as 'soon', in your area?
c What range of visibility is described in weather forecasts as poor?
d What conclusions would you reach if your barometer reading had been falling steadily at a rate of 2.5 m Bar per hour for the last two hours?
e What causes a sea breeze and when does it occur?
f What causes a katabatic wind?

g Name three factors, other than weather, which would influence a decision to put to sea or not, with a well found craft.

h What sea state, wave heights and wind speed prevail, when the wind is stated to be Force 4?

Answers to Chapter 13

Exercise 1

a Low temperature; low moisture content; small temperature gradient, with height.

b Tropical maritime; tropical continental.

c Towards higher latitudes.

d A high pressure area.

Exercise 2

a Winds will be steady and visibility will gradually deteriorate and persistent rain will commence, becoming heavy; the temperature will be steady but the pressure will fall quite rapidly. This weather will last until the warm front passes through. At that time the wind will veer to and freshen; the pressure will remain steady and the temperature will rise. The rain will then ease but the sky will remain overcast.

b As the front approaches rain will commence and become very heavy, the wind will freshen and veer. The pressure will rise sharply and the temperature will fall, as the cold front passes through. Behind the cold front, the pressure will rise slowly, the temperature will steady and visibility will become good.

c The wind will: **i** back, **ii** become cyclonic, **iii** veer.

d Barometer, thermometer, wind speed and direction, sea state, cloud formations.

Exercise 3

a Radio broadcasts, newspapers, television, telephone, Marinecall, VHF Ch 28.

b Between 6 and 12 hours.

c 1100 yds to 2 nautical miles.

d There is a strong possibility of an approaching gale.

e This occurs on a summer's day when the dry land is heated more quickly than the sea. The warm air over the land rises and air is drawn in from the sea to replace it. The day starts with a gentle onshore breeze which increases markedly during the day, probably dying out in the late afternoon.

f On a clear night adjacent to mountains with steep valleys between them, air is drawn down into the valleys as they cool and flows out to sea as a strong offshore breeze.

g Tides, depth of water, the sea bed, crew strength, and boat strength.

h Small waves, fairly frequent white horses; 1 m average, 1.5 m max; 11–16 kts.

118

14

Passage planning

The object of passage planning is to enable the various options for a voyage to be studied and a decision made on whether to proceed or not, based upon the assessment of all the relevant and available information. The information to be assessed includes:

- The proposed destination.

- The capability of the boat.

- The capability of the crew.

- Transport and access to the boat.

- Food, water, fuel, stores and supplies.

- Personal kit, clothing and bedding.

- Navigation equipment, charts, pilots and tidal data etc.

- Weather information and equipment.

Much of this work can be done ashore and a successful voyage is dependent upon good and adequate preparation. Let us consider each of the tasks outlined above, in turn.

Proposed Destination

Small scale charts are used for this initially. The approximate distance between departure and destination points is measured and an estimate of the voyage time is obtained. The actual time will of course be determined by the performance of the boat and the weather, but an estimated average boat speed of say 4 kts will enable a preliminary estimate of the voyage time to be calculated. Remember however that a sailing cruiser is unlikely to sail closer to the wind than 45° and her effective speed to windward is only about seven tenths of her logged speed, eg 45° off course at 6 kts = 4.2 kts on course. Now consider the effects of the tide. A 30 mile voyage at 4 kts will take about 7.5 hours. Such a voyage will best be achieved by carrying a fair tide for the maximum possible period of time. On a basis of a 6 hour flood and a 6 hour ebb, a foul tide for 1.5 hours would in this case be encountered. Much of course depends upon location; in some areas the flood lasts for 7 hours and the ebb only 5 hours. These local effects are addressed more closely in the detailed planning. The information so far obtained enables a decision to be made as to whether the proposed voyage is feasible. Now let us consider the details.

Capability of the Boat

The first question that arises is; is the vessel suitable for such a voyage? This can only be answered by considering the vessel's expected performance, seaworthiness and equipment. Each aspect has to be separately addressed. Some idea of her sailing performance needs to be obtained in order to estimate an average speed. Her seaworthiness is dependent upon her design and general condition. The content, quality and serviceability of her equipment needs to be thoroughly considered; with special attention paid to safety equipment, sails, rigging and anchor gear.

Capability of the Crew

The crew's capability must never be overlooked. Many people are affected by seasickness and this is most debilitating. Some vessels require greater crew strength for sailing handling and anchor work etc, than others. A long voyage will need to be adequately crewed and watches must be set to ensure that the crew are properly rested and fed. Another important factor is personality. Most sailing people have a common bond (other than survival) and mix well and easily but, in a small sailing craft minor irritations do arise; living and working together amicably is essential. To promote and ensure this harmony is the lot of the skipper.

It has been found that this is more easily achieved when the crew are given responsibility for some specific tasks and equipment. To this end, prepare in advance some check lists and give one of these to each crew member before going aboard. His task is then to familiarise him or herself with the location, function and operation of all the items on the list and in consequence, becomes the 'expert' on that particular feature of the boat. Typical examples of such lists are given below;

Sails and Deck Gear

- Identify what sails there are, where they are stowed and in which bags.
- Determine which halyards do what and how the reefing gear works.
- Locate the winch handles, fenders and warps.
- Check that the anchor gear works and that there is a spare anchor.
- Check the standing and running rigging, the guard rails and lifelines etc.

Safety Equipment

- Check the liferaft (but obviously NOT to inflate it).
- Issue to each crew member, a life harness and life jacket.
- Check the number, type and expiry date of the flares.
- Check the fire extinguishers and fire blankets.
- Check the life buoys and dan-buoy, including the operation of lifebuoy lights etc.

Navigation Equipment

- Check and list the charts. Ascertain whether they are up-to-date and cover the proposed cruising area.
- Check the operation of instruments and the availability of chartwork instruments.
- Check the operation of navigation lights, the VHF set and the broadcast receiver for weather forecasts, etc.
- Check the availability and publication dates of pilots, almanacs, tide tables and tide stream atlases.

The Engine and the Toilet

- Check the engine, its controls, fuel, oil, the cooling arrangement and the location of all sea cocks. Run the engine and ensure that all is well.
- Check the state of the batteries.
- Check the location and contents of the tool box and engine spares.
- Check the location of the spare fuel can and its contents.
- Check the outboard engine and its spare fuel and oil cans.
- Check and test the operation of the toilet, the location and function of its seacocks and the arrangements for drainage. (Toilet compartments do not normally drain into the bilges).

- Check the supply of cleaning materials and toilet paper.

Galley and Cabin

- Check the stowage and location of all food and stores brought on board.
- Check the condition of the cooker, its gas hoses and the whereabouts and contents of all gas bottles.
- Prepare a menu and the first meal.
- Check the contents of the water tanks, top up as necessary.
- Check the availability of cleaning equipment, the whereabouts of all crockery, utensils and cutlery.

The above lists are a guideline, they are by no means mandatory, they have been developed over the years and they work, in that they give the crew an immediate sense of purpose from the outset. There are obviously other ways to do this, it is a matter of preference for the skipper.

Transport and Access to the Boat

If you are already aboard then this matter is resolved. If you are planning a voyage from home or elsewhere however it must be properly organised. Transport arrangements must be made for the crew, their kit and the food. This is generally best done at a preliminary meeting, especially if the crew are from different places. Arrangements to rendezvous near to the mooring must be made and it is sensible to ensure that parking arrangements exist. It is also prudent to address the problem of return journeys in the event that it may not be possible to return to your point of departure, by reason of damage, the weather or some other cause. This is particularly important when a voyage to a foreign port is being planned.

If the vessel is moored on piles or at a buoy, then access will probably be by dinghy. In this event, take extra care; do not overload the dinghy and ensure that oilskins, sea boots and lifejackets are worn.

Food, Water, Fuel, Stores and Supplies

The amount of food taken will depend upon the numbers of the crew. Sailing seems to generate large appetites. It is sensible to provide for this, too much rather than not enough. Ensure whenever possible that the crew get a good hot meal before sailing and, in addition to providing hot meals, make up sandwich packs and put hot soup into vacuum flasks, so that food can be provided under sail without the need for too much work in the galley. Provide plenty of fruit, biscuits and mini chocolate bars (Mars, Topics and Bountys etc); in fact anything that is nourishing and can be eaten with one hand. Supplies should include a good selection of tinned food, sufficient to last about three days; more on long voyages. Be sure however to indelibly mark the tins to indicate their contents; if nothing else, this avoids putting peaches into the soup! Provide a good selection of soft drinks as well as the more usual tea, coffee and cocoa. Alcoholic drinks are a matter for the skipper to decide upon. My rule is, that the spirit locker is not opened until we have a line ashore; this rule is based on the assumption that enough things can go wrong whilst sailing without adding to them (it also speeds up the operation of mooring!)

The problem of diets (the allergic type) could also arise and this information should be obtained beforehand.

Water supplies must be located ashore to top up the tanks; don't forget to flush the hose first. Add 'Aquatabs' or even a very small teaspoonful of household bleach, if you are uncertain of the purity of the water.

Keep the fuel tank well topped up to reduce the effects of condensation and hence water in the fuel.

Provide spare dry batteries for torches, lifebuoy lights, the radio and the RDF set etc. Have at least two torches on board, waterproof if possible and encourage the crew to carry a small personal torch. One of these might well save a life in a man overboard situation at night.

Ensure that all stores brought on board are stowed away securely and that somebody has a list of what is stowed and where. Dry goods need to be properly wrapped to keep them dry and matches are best stored in at least two places.

Personal kit, Clothing and Bedding

The crew should be encouraged to list what they intend to take with them. Some take very little, others the kitchen sink! It all, however, has to be stowed away and this needs to be emphasised. In addition to the usual washing kit, a complete change of clothes is essential, together with a good supply of thick sweaters. Lots of layers of clothing are more efficient in retaining body heat than a single thick garment. Each crew member must also be equipped with a good set of oilskins, large enough to go over a well-clad body without being too tight. A good pair of sea boots with non-slip soles and a hat complete the picture; don't forget the hat, heat loss from the head is greater than from other parts of the body.

Bedding usually consists of sleeping bags. Keep these dry when you are not in them, by wrapping them in a plastic or other waterproof bag.

Seasickness is not easy to cure and it is not pleasant to endure. Carry some remedial medicine in your personal kit. I recommend a 'Stugeron' tablet with breakfast and more during the day if needed; keep to the maker's instructions though!

Navigation Equipment, Charts, Pilots, Almanacs and Tidal Data

Check the contents of the chart table and ensure that the charts needed for the voyage are up-to-date. Consult the pilot books and the almanac and makes notes relevant to the ports to be visited. Check that the tide tables are up-to-date and that the appropriate tidal atlases are available. If you intend to use the vessel's chartwork instruments, make sure that those you need are available and in good condition. Finally check over the compass and locate the deviation card. Check the hand bearing compass, the RDF set, the VHF set and whatever other navigational aids are on board. Check that the vessel's log and depth-sounder are working.

Weather Information and Equipment

Ensure that you can receive the weather forecast and examine the last forecast issued. It is prudent to record forecasts and to retain copies of those for the last few days. These will enable a 'feel' for the weather to be obtained and can help in drawing a synoptic chart from a radio broadcast. Check the serviceability of the barometer and thermometer; this is not easy and generally requires numerous recorded observations. Beware the barometer that never changes!!

Exercise 1

a List the matters that need to be addressed before setting out on a passage.
b What arrangements are made on a long voyage to enable the crew to be fed and rested?
c What documents would you essentially require on a 50-mile passage?
d If your vessel is capable on a reach of a sustained 5 knots in a force 4 breeze, what speed would you expect to make windward when sailing close hauled?
e What safety equipment would you carry on a 50-mile off-shore passage?

The Passage Plan

Having established that the vessel is ready and equipped, detailed consideration to the passage itself can now be contemplated. Let us draw up a plan to sail from the Grand Lejon lighthouse to Jersey (St Helier) on July 29th.

The tidal data for Dover is as follows:

Time zone GMT	h mins	m
Dover	0428	5.5
Tu July	1123	2.0
29	1647	5.7
Neaps	0000	2.0 (Jul 30)

High Water St Helier is about 5 hours after HW Dover.

Routes   Using the Stanford Channel Islands chart.

An examination of the chart shows that a direct route can be taken and that the distance to sail is about 35 miles. At 5 knots the sailing time will be about 7 hours. The pilot states that St Helier is accessible at all states of the tide but that the marina gates open at 3.5 hours before high water and close at 3.5 hours afterwards. Examination of the tidal stream atlas (TSA) (at the end of the chapter) shows that the tide runs fair (easterly) at St Helier until about 5 hours before high water and turns at 4 hours before. We could therefore time our arrival for about 1200 GMT ie HW − 4.47.

Tides   Now consider the tides, so as to determine the departure time and best course to steer from Grand Léjon. We have decided (above) that it is best to arrive at 1200, assuming a 7-hour voyage, our time of departure would be 0500; half an hour after high water. We therefore examine the TSA sheet for HW + 1 initially as this will prevail from 0458 until 0558. To simplify calculation we will assume 0500–0600. At that time the tide at Grand Léjon is setting NW at 0.2 knots. One hour later and 5 miles closer to St Helier the tide is slack and an hour after that, it is setting east at 1 knot. It remains to determine the tidal set and rate for each hour of the voyage. The position on the TSA sheet at which the tidal information is taken, obviously corresponds to the vessel's estimated position at that time, ie 4 hours after departure her position would be 4/7th of the total distance. To avoid confusion it is prudent to set out the tidal values obtained in a simple table as shown below.

	(From the tidal data above)		
Time	TSA sheet	Set	Rate
1st HW 0428			
0500–0600	HW + 1	NW	0.2
0600–0700	HW + 2	Slack	
0700–0800	HW + 3	E	1.0
0800–0900	HW + 4	ESE	2.6
0900–1000	HW + 5	E	3.0
1000–1100	HW + 6	E	2.2
2nd HW 1647			
1020–1120	HW − 6	E	1.6
1120–1220	HW − 5	E	0.6

Course to Steer

To determine the course to steer one would normally:

a Plot the required ground track, by joining the point of departure and destination.

b Plot the individual tidal vectors for each of the 7 hours of the voyage and,

c Strike an arc of 35 miles (7 hours at 5 knots) to intersect the ground track; the resulting vector being the course to steer.

For the purpose of planning the passage however, we are merely trying to establish the departure time and course to steer.

Let us therefore address each of the above points in turn and plot the vectors at each stage.

a The Ground Track — Mark this on the chart, making allowance for any deviation in course posed by obvious hazards. (Stage 1 — Plot this vector. A useful tip here when drawing a vector of greater length than your parallel rule is to extend the parallel rule by placing against it, edge to edge, an ordinary ruler. By sliding the ruler along the edge of the parallel rule, the points of departure and destination can be aligned and so enable the ground track to be drawn accurately.)

b The Tidal Vectors — In areas of strong tidal streams, it is not easy to predict these with accuracy. Examination of the table above reveals that there is a small set NW of 0.2 kts for an hour and for most of the remaining time between 0700 and 1100 the tide sets easterly. It is quite reasonable for the purpose of this estimate to regard the ESE vector as an E vector. The effective tidal set between 0500 and 1100 is therefore the sum of those values and is equal to 8.8 knots and flows in an Easterly direction.

For the period of time between 1100 and 1200 the effective set will still be easterly but only for 1/3rd (20 mins) of the HW $-$ 6 value. ie $1.6 \div 3 \fallingdotseq 0.5$ and for 2/3rds (40 mins) of the HW $-$ 5 value. ie $0.6 \times 2/3 - = 0.4$. The effective set between 1100 and 1200 is then $0.5 + 0.4 = 0.9$ East.

The total effective set is therefore $8.8 + 0.9 = 9.7$M East. (Stage 2 — Plot this vector.)

c Course to Steer — The tidal vector East 9.7M is then plotted on the chart from the Grand Léjon lighthouse and the distance, from its end, to St Helier is measured. This will be found to be about 28 miles.

At 5 knots this distance will be covered in 5 hrs 40 mins. We had originally allowed 7 hours for the voyage but the tidal lift obtained will enable us to complete the voyage more rapidly and we can therefore leave 1 hr 20 mins later ie, at 0620.

The tidal vector would normally be adjusted to allow for this but, as can be seen from the table, the tide for the 1st hour sets NW and that was ignored and for the second hour the tide was slack and that can also be ignored. The tidal vector thus remains 9.7M. NB (In practice things do not always work out so conveniently).

It remains therefore to strike an arc corresponding to 28 miles in length, ie 5 h 40 m sailing, which intersects the ground track. Then read off the bearing of the resulting course. (Stage 3 — Plot this vector.) This will be found to be 026°T. NB It is unlikely that your dividers will span the distance scaled for 28 m. It is sufficiently, accurate in passage planning however to measure the distance with a ruler and to use that length and the ruler to strike the arc.

Summary

To summarise, we can leave Grand Léjon lighthouse at 0620 on 29 July and to steer 026°T heading for St Helier at an average speed of 5 knots. Our ETA is 1200.

Waypoints

To check the progress of the voyage it is prudent to establish certain points en route against which progress can be measured. These are waypoints. On this particular voyage the most obvious choice is the NW Minquiers buoy.

Summary

The objective of passage planning is to relieve the navigator of as much work as is possible whilst at sea. This is achieved by:

- Adequate preparation in respect of, compiling easily read and understood notes and calculations, prior to sailing.

- Ensuring that charts and nautical publications are up-to-date and adequate for the voyage and; for harbours and anchorages, of the largest scale possible.

- Studying the intended passage on the chart and laying off approximate tracks, working from small scale to large scale charts. These plans will have to be modified whilst in passage, but they are a useful guide to navigational marks and dangers.

- Adjusting the sailing time (time of departure) so that the tidal stream is favourable for as much of the passage as possible, particularly in areas where tidal streams are fast.

- Taking account of weather forecasts. The possibility of delaying departure must always be considered in the event of an unfavourable forecast.

- Planning to keep clear of dangers, but making optimum use of shallow water to avoid commercial shipping, especially in fog. Make alternative plans in case foul weather should occur on passage; it is important to know **in advance** where refuge can be found and how long it will take to reach. Having made a plan for the voyage, enter the details into a work-book into which other calculations can be entered as they arise on passage.

- Ensuring that whenever possible the crew are given a hot meal prior to sailing. They may not be able to have a hot meal at sea in rough conditions.

The Ship's Log

To ensure the safe navigation of any ship, it is essential that an accurate log book be kept. Entries should be made hourly. The function of a log is to provide a record of courses and distances to enable an estimated position (EP), to be 'worked up'. Weather conditions should also be recorded in respect of barometric pressure, temperature, and speed and direction.

Exercise 2

Use the Stanford Channel Islands chart.

a At what time in the passage planned from Grand Léjon LH to St Helier, above, will NW Minquiers buoy be abeam?

b What is the approximate length of the route, passing west of the Plateau des Minquiers, from St Malo to St Helier?

c What is the approximate length of the route, passing east of the Plateau des Minquiers, from St Malo to St Helier?

d What would be the approximate sailing time over each route at 5 knots assuming no 'tide lift'?

e Draw up a list of the tides for a 9 hour passage passing east of the Plateau des Minquiers, between St Malo and St Helier. Start at HW + 2.

f Draw up a list of the tides for a 9 hour passage passing west of the Plateau des Minquiers, between St Malo and St Helier. Start at HW − 4.

g Which is the preferred route? State your reasons.

Answers to
Chapter 14

Exercise 1

a The proposed destination.
   The capability of the boat.
   The capability of the crew.
   Transport and access to the boat.
   Food, water, fuel, stores and supplies.
   Personal kit, clothing and bedding.
   Navigation equipment, charts, pilots and tidal data etc.
   Weather information and equipment.

b Watches are set and the crew divided so that one crew is on watch whilst the other rests.

c Charts, almanacs, tide tables, tidal stream atlases and pilot books.

d 3.5 knots.

e Lifejackets and harnesses for everyone on board. Liferaft capable of carrying everyone on board. Flarepack comprising 4 red parachute flares, 4 red hand flares, 2 orange smoke candles and 2 white hand flares.

Exercise 2

a 0942. [At 0920 (3 hrs after departure) the tidal set will have been 4.6 m East ie 1 M from 0700–0800, 2.6 M from 0800–0900 and 1 M from 0900–0920 3 hrs sailing at 5 kts will give an EP about 2.3 M WSW of the buoy. The ground track to that EP scales 17.4 M giving a ground speed of 5.8 kts. The distance from Grand Lejon to the buoy is 19.5 M and thus at a ground speed of 5.8 kts the time to the buoy is 3.36 hrs (3 h 22 m) ∴ ETA at the buoy is then 0620 + 3 hr 22 m = 0942.]

b 41M

c 43M

d Just under 9 hours.

e Tidal data for the route East of the Minquiers.

Hr	Time	Set	Rate
1	HW + 2	Slack	
2	+ 3	E	1.0
3	+ 4	E/S	1.6
4	+ 5	E	2.0
5	+ 6	ENE	1.8
6	HW − 5	N/E	0.6
7	− 4	NW	0.6
8	− 3	NW	1.4
9	− 2	NW	2.2

f Tidal Data for the route West of the Minquiers.

Hr	Time	Set	Rate
1	HW − 4	NW	0.2
2	− 3	W	1.0
3	− 2	W	1.7
4	− 1	W	1.2
5	HW	W	1.6
6	+ 1	W	1.1
7	+ 2	SW	0.5
8	+ 3	SE	1.0
9	+ 4	SE	2.4

g The NE route will benefit from a greater tidal lift. It would not however be prudent in rough weather.

Appendices

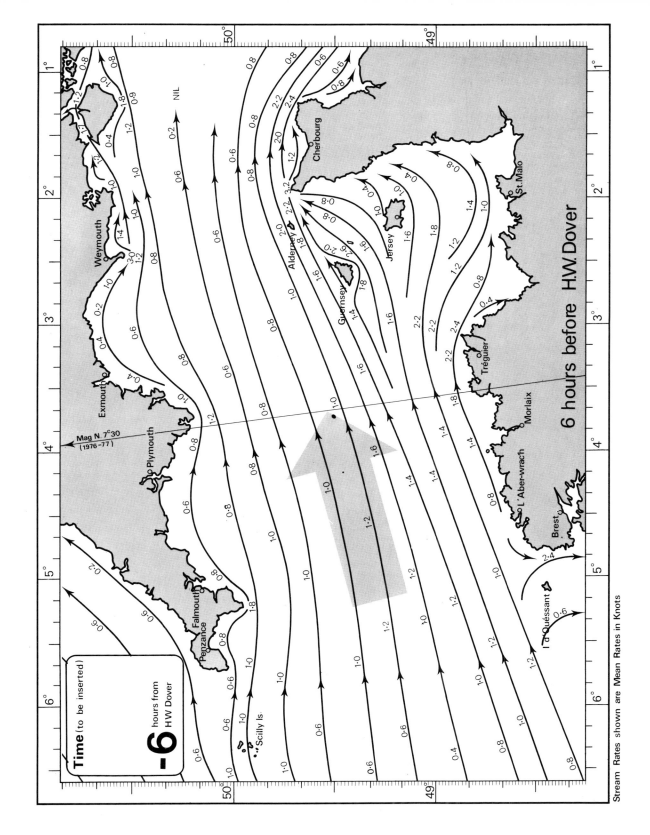

6 hours before H.W. Dover

Stream Rates shown are Mean Rates in Knots

Time (to be inserted)
-6 hours from H.W. Dover

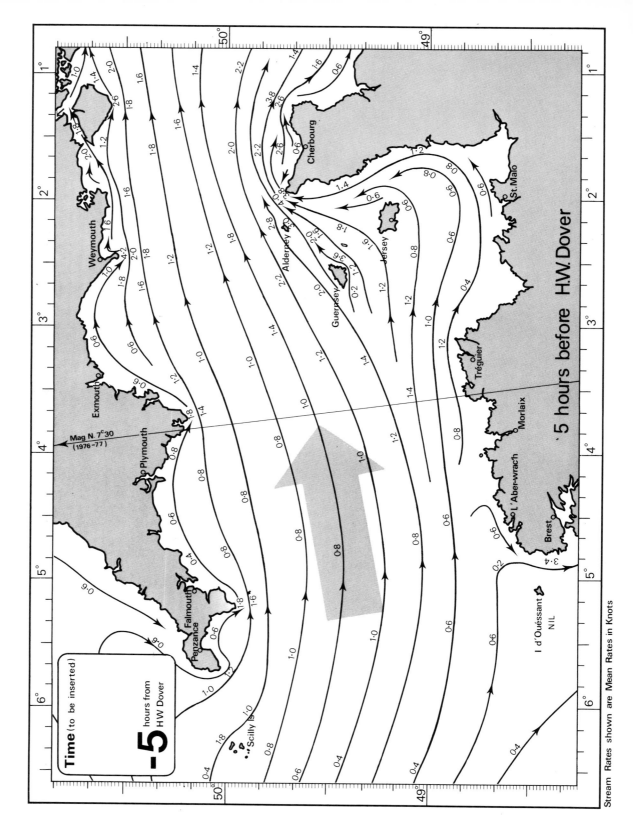

Time (to be inserted)

-5 hours from HW Dover

·5 hours before H.W. Dover

Stream Rates shown are Mean Rates in Knots

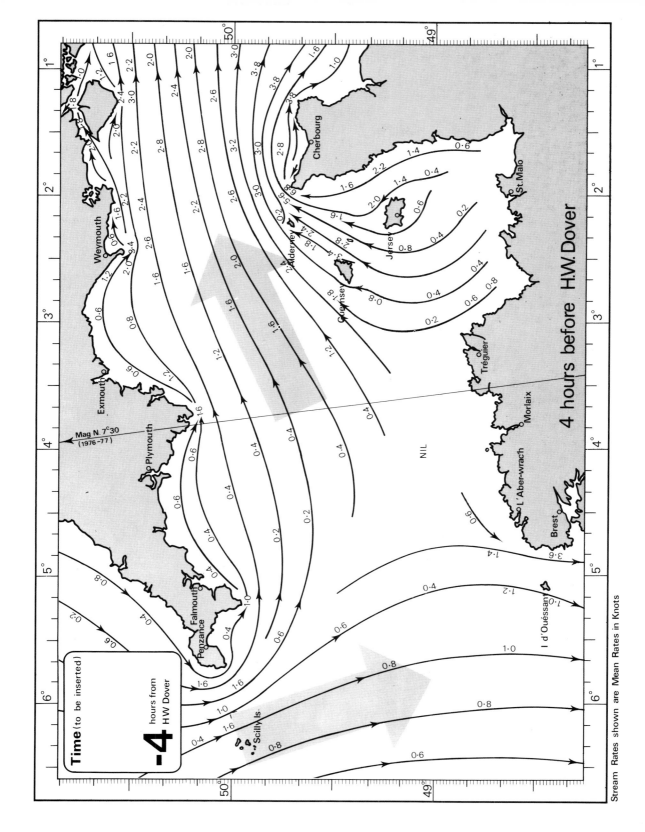

4 hours before H.W. Dover

Stream Rates shown are Mean Rates in Knots

Time (to be inserted)

-4 hours from HW Dover

133

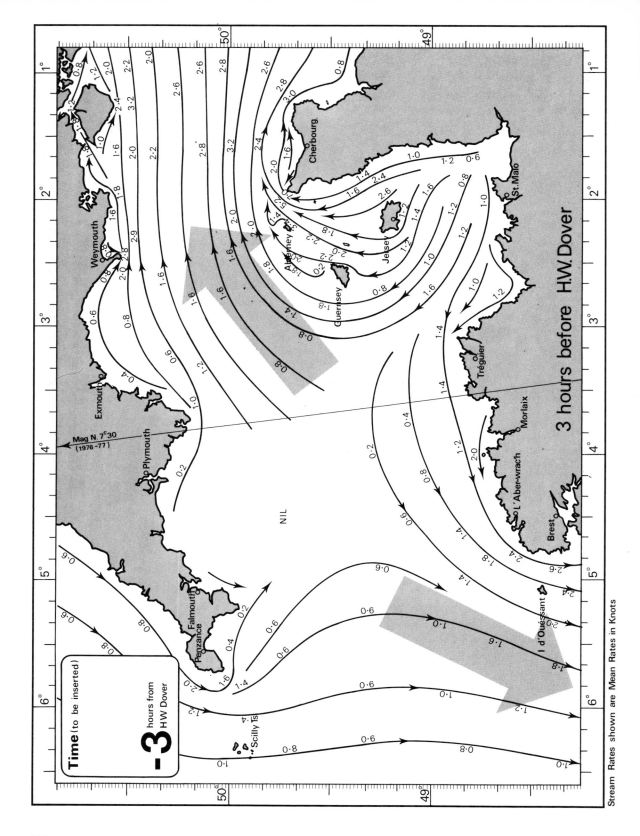

Time (to be inserted)

−3 hours from HW Dover

3 hours before HW. Dover

Stream Rates shown are Mean Rates in Knots

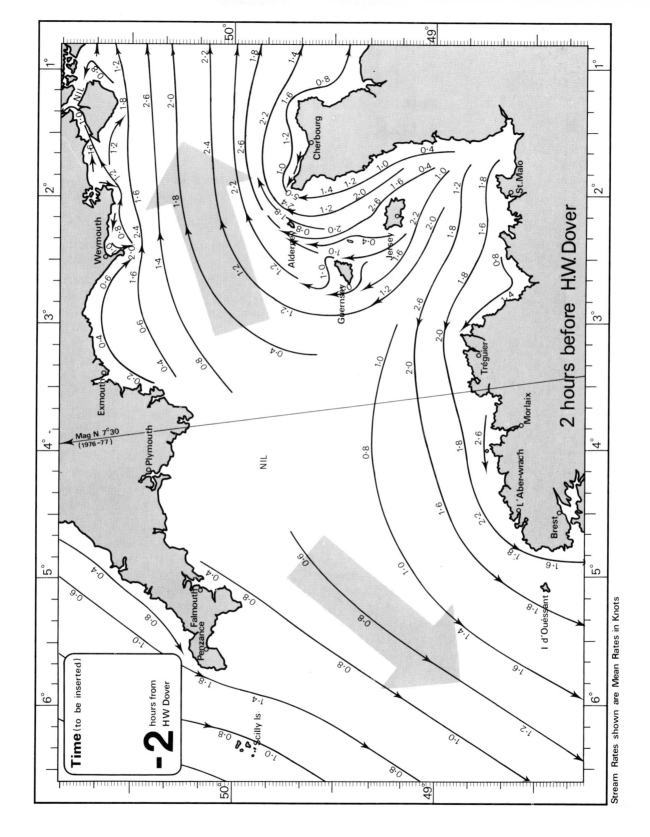

2 hours before H.W. Dover

Time (to be inserted)

-2 hours from HW Dover

Stream Rates shown are Mean Rates in Knots

135

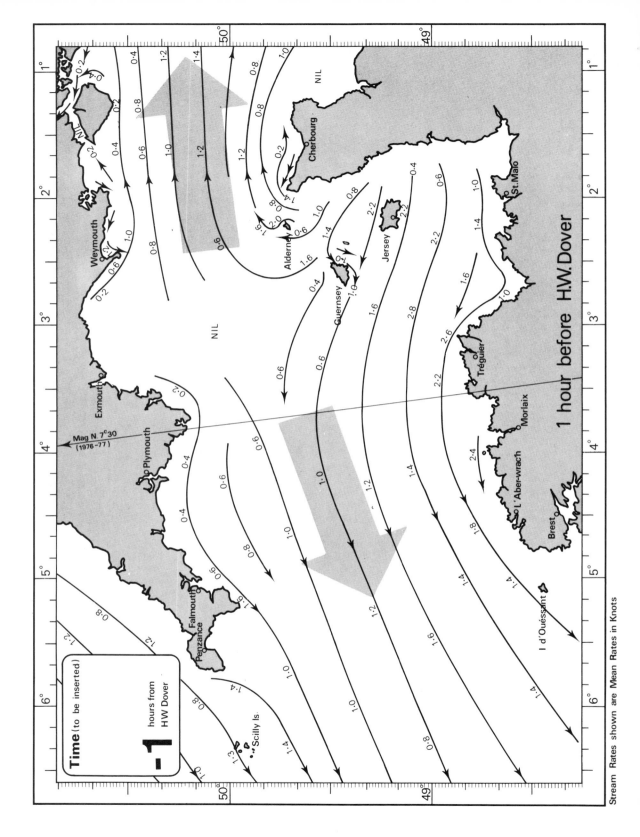

1 hour before H.W. Dover

Stream Rates shown are Mean Rates in Knots

Time (to be inserted)

1 hours from HW Dover

136

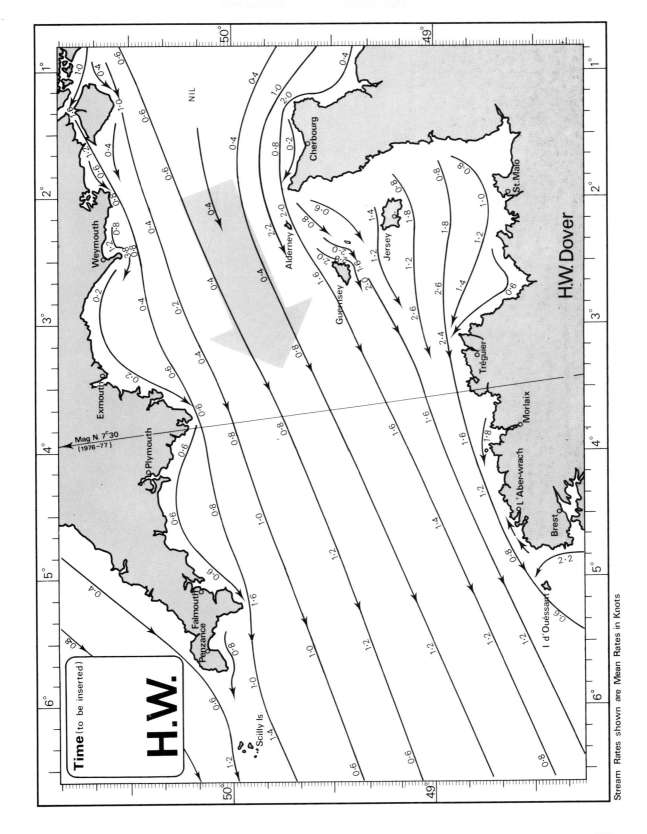

Time (to be inserted)

H.W.

H.W. Dover

Stream Rates shown are Mean Rates in Knots

Mag N 7°30
(1976-77)

NIL

Weymouth
Exmouth
Plymouth
Falmouth
Penzance
Scilly Is.
Cherbourg
Alderney
Guernsey
Jersey
St.Malo
Tréguier
Morlaix
L'Aber-wrach
Brest
I d'Ouéssant

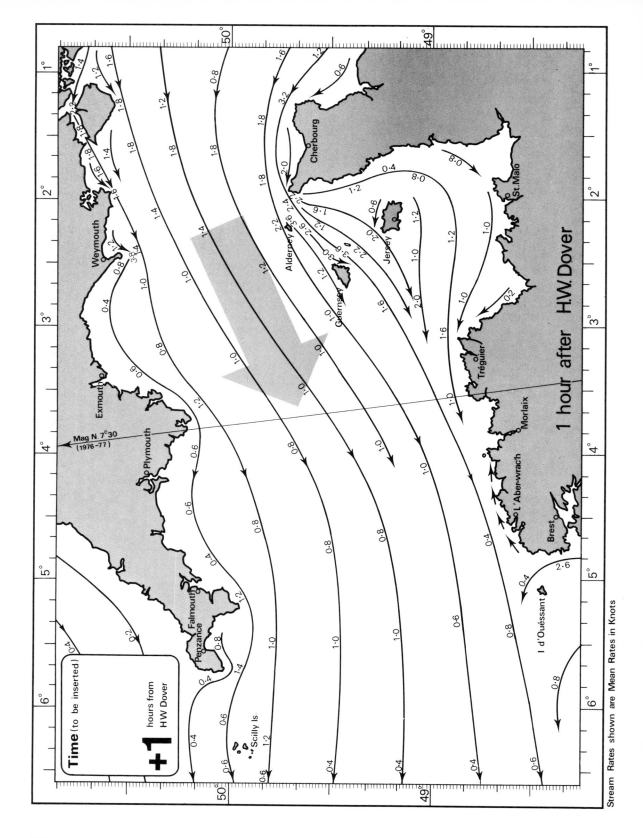

1 hour after H.W.Dover

Mag N. 7°30 (1976−77)

Time (to be inserted)

+1 hours from HW Dover

Stream Rates shown are Mean Rates in Knots

138

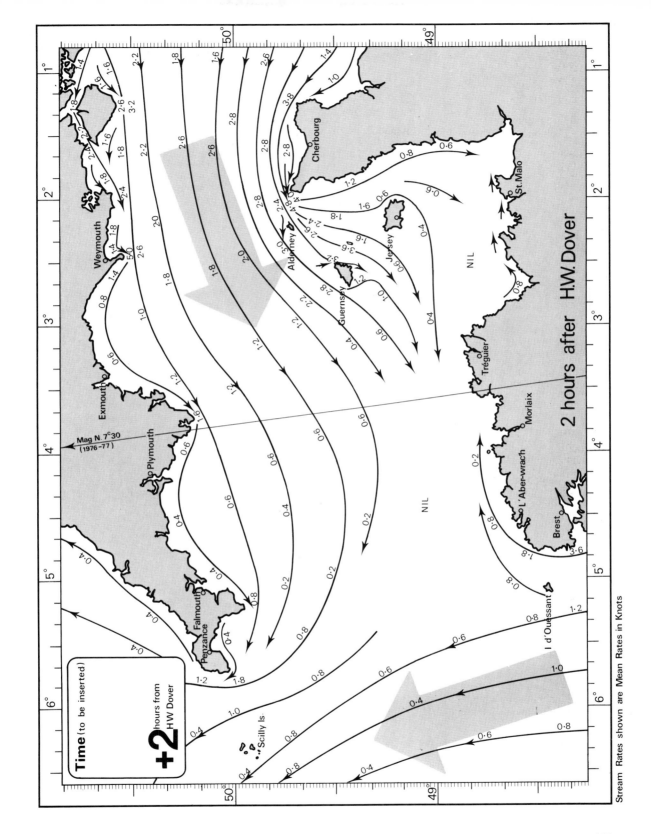

2 hours after H.W. Dover

Mag. N. 7°30 (1976-77)

Time (to be inserted)

+2 hours from HW Dover

Stream Rates shown are Mean Rates in Knots

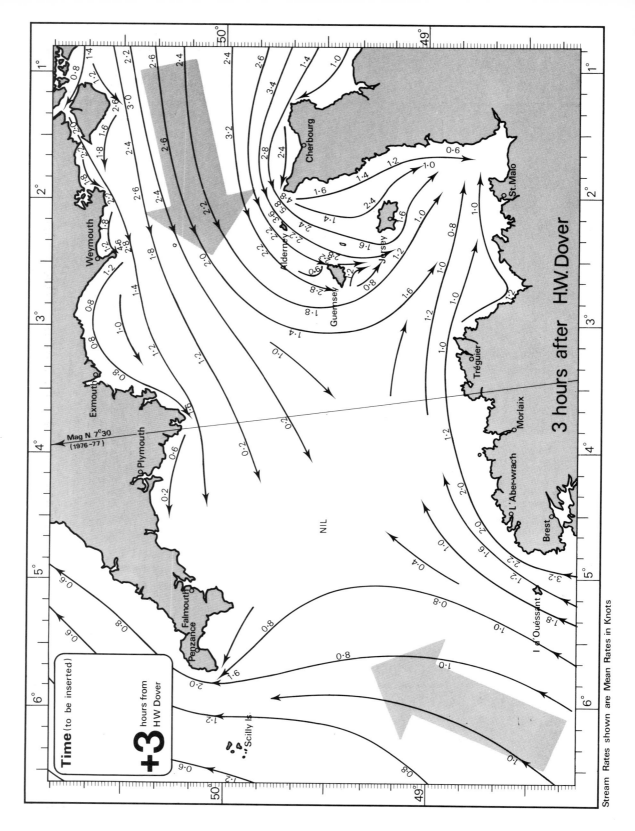

3 hours after H.W. Dover

Time (to be inserted)

+3 hours from H.W Dover

Stream Rates shown are Mean Rates in Knots

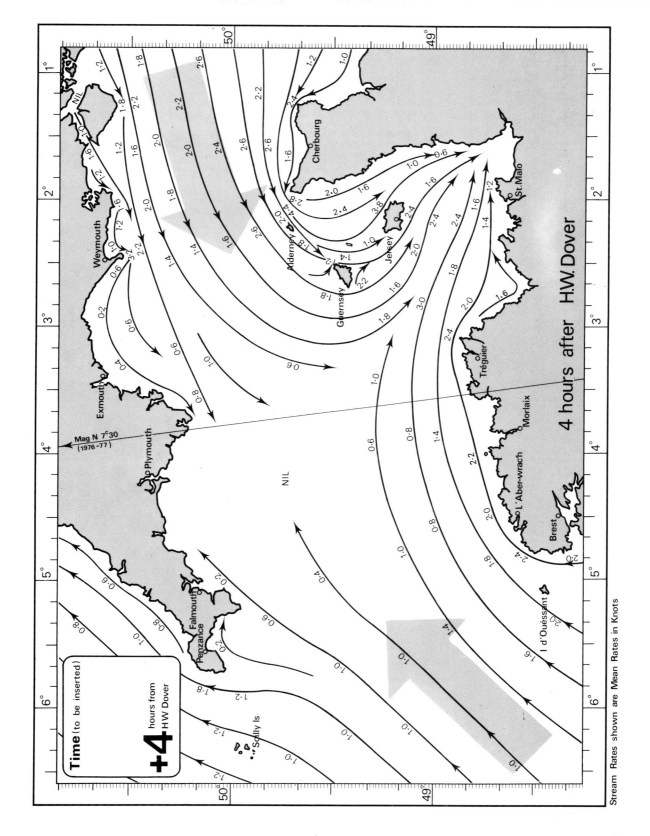

Time **(to be inserted)**

+4 hours from H.W Dover

4 hours after H.W. Dover

Stream Rates shown are Mean Rates in Knots

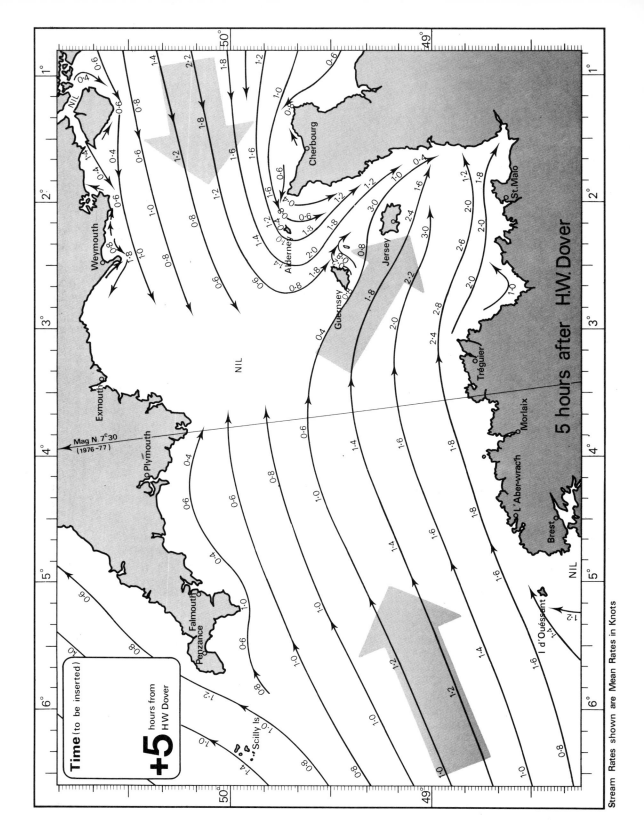

5 hours after H.W. Dover

Time (to be inserted)

+5 hours from HW Dover

Stream Rates shown are Mean Rates in Knots

142

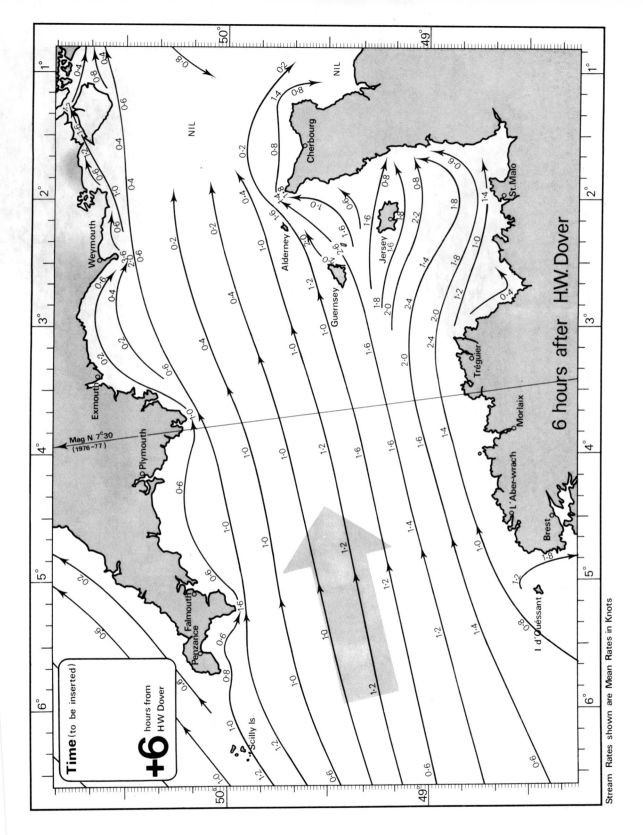

6 hours after H.W. Dover

Time (to be inserted)

+6 hours from H.W Dover

Stream Rates shown are Mean Rates in Knots